LUDLOW *at leisure*

a country town at play 1800-1950

Derek Beattie

MERLIN UNWIN BOOKS

First published in the UK by Merlin Unwin Books Ltd, 2020

Merlin Unwin Books Ltd
Palmers House
7 Corve Street
Ludlow, Shropshire SY8 1DB
www.merlinunwin.co.uk

The author asserts his moral right to be identified with this work.

ISBN 978-1-913159-21-4

Typeset in 12 point Bembo by Merlin Unwin Books
Printed by TJ International, Padstow, England

Previous page: Bentfield Hucks lands his Bleriot monoplane in front of 4,000 paying spectators at Ludford Park, 1913.

Opposite page: Ludlow Boating Club had exclusive rights to enjoy the waters above Dinham Weir thanks to Lord Windsor.
(Courtesy of Lottie James)

For Judith
who gave me over fifty years
of happiness

Contents

ACKNOWLEDGEMENTS

My thanks to the staff at Ludlow Library and Shropshire Archives for their kind help and also to the members of the Ludlow History Research Group for their constant support. Special thanks must go to Roy Payne for reading the manuscript and suggesting amendments, most of which I happily took on board, and to Phil Williams for his careful work improving and enhancing many of the historic photos in this book, including the front cover image.

Grateful thanks also must go to Merlin and Karen for their support in the publishing of local historical research.

In 1924 the town saw its first Brownie pack formed. (Courtesy of Pam Walters)

CHAPTER ONE

The Attack on Tradition

Over the centuries and throughout the length and breadth of the country, leisure pursuits evolved only slowly. However, as the pace of change altered with the rapid movement of population from the countryside to the towns and cities that came about with the Industrial Revolution, together with the rise of a new middle-class wanting to define its own place in society, this would alter. The result was rapid social change, and that included leisure pursuits.

With the Municipal Reform Act, the demise of the ruling Corporation and the rise to power of the new borough council in 1836, Ludlow saw the beginning of the end of country house government. The political power of the local aristocracy and gentry, who for centuries had dominated the town, slowly began to decline. In its place came the rise to influence of the new middle-classes: men from the professions, and an emergent shopocracy made up of the leading tradesmen. The result was that leisure patterns in Ludlow would now undergo change as this growing urban elite took up their own new pursuits, whilst at the same time, imbued with Victorian morality, they attempted to mould the ways that the bulk of the townsfolk enjoyed themselves. Meanwhile, in the surrounding countryside, traditional rural pursuits also came under pressure to change.

Fieldsports

Pastimes that failed to survive were those that were deemed too cruel. With the rising influence of an urban middle-class elite in Parliament, the Cruelty to Animals Act 1835 saw sports such as cock fighting, dog fighting, bear baiting and badger baiting, whose local supporters crossed social barriers, all made illegal. That is not to say that they totally disappeared, for underground activity in such sports did continue.

In 1860, before a large gathering, a 30lb badger was turned out of a bag in a field off the Caynham Road. Amidst heavy betting, fifteen terrier dogs were released to fight it. What happened next was fully reported in a local newspaper. It appears that the badger initially did well and 'some hearty

Badger baiting was a sport popular with all social classes and was accompanied by heavy betting. A badger was turned loose amongst a pack of dogs to see how long it could survive and how many of its attackers it could maim in the process.

shakes were given and the dogs dreadfully lacerated.' The badger broke away and a chase ensued even after the badger had swum a stream. Then, after two startled hares sidetracked the dogs, the badger escaped much to the dismay of the organiser who had paid 14/- for it. Though this whole escapade was illegal it is interesting to note that the article made no mention of this and displayed no hint of criticism of the day's events, almost certainly reflecting the readership's views.

Shades of badger baiting could still be discerned fifty years later. On the Peaton Hall estate in the early twentieth century, when a sett was dug out, the badgers, instead of being shot, had the dogs set on them. The adult male badger, after apparently putting up a good fight, was killed by a collie sheep dog and a terrier, as was his female mate and three cubs. Once again the newspaper article contained no hint of criticism[1].

Cock fighting, even though it became illegal in 1835, apparently carried on quite openly in Ludlow until about 1849. A number of public houses had a cockpit, including the *Feathers* on Corve Steet and the *Mug House* on Old Street that was situated on the north side of Friars Walk. (This inn saw a number of changes of name. When it closed down in the 1880s it was called the *Friars Inn*.)[2] Once again this sport never totally died out as it just went underground and a number of court cases followed illegal meetings throughout the border counties. Such contests were still taking place in the 1930s. Sir James Croft of Croft Castle was a keen follower and participant as his niece recalled:

> *'My uncle, Jimmy Croft, was very keen on cockfighting. He not only did cockfighting but also used his employees to help him and one chap who worked here told me that they went to a cockfight and they were in the back of a car and they had to stop at Ludlow where the road goes over the top of a hill and two policemen (were) standing there. When the car started up the fighting cocks started crowing all at once. They were terrified they'd given the game away. Luckily the police don't seem to have noticed.'*[3]

However, many fieldsports remained legal. These were ones that were thought to give the animal a sporting chance of survival. Such sports remained a fixture in the countryside and were widely supported by the local aristocracy and gentry. Foxhunting was one example. This had always gone on but it became formalised c.1760. By the 1850s the local pack was registered as the Ludlow Hunt with Boodle's Club of Pall Mall, the body that drew up the foxhunting rules and settled any disputes. The area hunted encompassed about a ten-mile radius surrounding Ludlow and hunts took place up to four times a week in the season. Sir William Curtis of Caynham Court held the post of Master of the Hunt between 1886 and 1907 and it was he who constructed purpose-built kennels adjacent to his property and moved the pack from Wetmore.[4] The annual Boxing Day Meet that assembled at Ludlow Castle also survived intact and still takes place to this day, continuing to draw in hundreds of onlookers. Except for the first two years of the Great War, foxhunting went on its uninterrupted way until well into the twentieth century.

Other fieldsports also carried on undisturbed. Packs of beagles to hunt hares were kept by a number of influential families. The Ludlow Foot Beagles were formed in 1875 and kept at the Bromfield racecourse. They met at Hope Court, Hope Bagot for their first outing. Sir William Curtis of Caynham Court purchased a pack in 1882 after coming down from Oxford University and kept them in kennels for four years at Catholic Hill, Caynham. The Seatons of Heath House, Clungunford, owned yet another pack. This met on the Old Field at Bromfield in 1891 and the hunt was followed by a 'large and fashionable attendance.'[5]

Otter hunts also had a wide following amongst the local gentry including, among many others, the families from Moor Park, Ludford House, Ashford Court, Stanage Park and Brampton Bryan. Such hunts attracted many foot followers both male and female, though by the 1890s a number of them

Foxhunting was a favourite sport for the local aristocracy and gentry whether as active members or as followers. The local hunt met throughout the nineteenth and twentieth centuries and their annual Boxing Day meet at Ludlow Castle constantly attracted large crowds. (Author's collection)

made use of bicycles. The Hawkstone Otter Hunt, that in 1903 kennelled its fifty hounds at Ludlow Racecourse, often met up to three times a week with each day's event being covered in the local newspapers. Chasing down an otter could take a number of hours before the animal was cornered by the chasing pack. One hunt that started at Downton Castle lasted 4½ hours before a large dog otter of 52lb was finally caught. Another hunt dislodged an otter from its holt near Diddlebury Bridge and it took 3½ hours before it was caught trying to cross a ford. Here 'a good fight took place, the otter fastening one of the hounds by the nose' before it was finally dispatched.[6] The Hawkstone Otter Hunt carried on undisturbed during the interwar years though its followers tended now to make use of

This Beagle pack, photographed at Caynham Court in 1886 and owned by Sir William Curtis, was one of a number that could be found locally. Using these dogs to hunt hares on foot was very popular and following a pack in action was a pastime that attracted many. (Courtesy of Shropshire Museum Service)

motorcars. In 1929 alone the Hunt enjoyed 75 outings, found 67 otters and scored 55 kills.[7] The Hunt was still in operation in the 1950s.

Rural fieldsports also had a following on a wider social scale. Hare coursing was seen at Oakley Park in 1862. Both the president and vice president of the organising body were local farmers: one from Stanton Lacy and the other from Bromfield. The meet saw a 'large company assembled' and a great number of dogs. Afterwards an evening meal followed by singing was held at the *Clive Arms Inn*. Forty years later the sport was still going strong and annual meets were being held at Onibury on the Stokesay Court estate and once again organised by tenant farmers. In 1906 'strong hares were found in plenty and contests (were) very keen.' Again the day's excitement ended with a dinner, this time at the *Stokesay Hotel* and also followed by singing.[8]

Attracting a following from even further down the social scale was rabbit coursing. The Ludlow Fox Terrier Coursing Society attracted the urban working-classes and not only as spectators but also as dog-owning participants. In 1890 the secretary and organiser was the landlord of the *Charlton Arms Hotel* and the meet was in Ludford Park, and the following years saw meets on the Burway and on land near the *Salwey Arms.* At one meeting in 1892 owners of winning dogs included a coach painter, a bricklayer's labourer, a fishmonger and a publican. Such gatherings could also be boisterous such as when three brothers from Ludlow were ejected from the inn for fighting after the meet had ended.[9]

This photograph, taken c1903, shows members of the local Hawkstone Hunt closing in to kill an otter that finally had been run to exhaustion by the dogs. The crowds lining the river bank indicates that following such hunts, that could last a few hours, was seen by many as a very enjoyable day out.

(Courtesy of Shropshire Museum Service)

Shooting sports were also popular. The upper classes enjoyed grouse shooting on the Long Mynd and the shooting of wild deer driven out of Whitcliffe Wood by beaters. For those further down the social scale, including rural workers and even tradesmen, there were organised pigeon shoots with the birds being released from traps. The landlord of the *Mitre Inn* on Corve Street organised such shoots in a field at Fishmore in the 1860s and 1870s with a pig as the prize, followed by a meal and a singsong back at the public house. The landlord of the *Nelson Inn* at Rocks Green held a similar meet on adjoining land in 1904. In 1914, the landlord of the *Exchange Vaults* organised a match at Ludford Park with the Receiving Officer of the Ludlow Workhouse as referee. Pigeons were released to be shot though it appears that, to the frustration of the competitors,

To ensure that wildlife was protected so that successful and productive shoots could be organised, gamekeepers were employed on all large estates. This group, assembled outside the head gamekeeper's cottage in 1912/13, were employed on the Oakley Park estate [today spelled Oakly] **on the edge of Ludlow.**
(Courtesy of Shropshire Museum Service)

Shooting was not the sole preserve of the upper classes. This group, that appears to be made up of local farmers, farmworkers and tradesmen, are enjoying a day hunting rabbits towards Craven Arms. (Courtesy of Shropshire Museum Service)

some refused to leave their cages. Nevertheless, 36 entrants had an enjoyable day and the winner was a land agent and farmer from Richards Castle. In addition, the Woofferton Amateur Gun Club held an annual shoot at the *Salwey Arms* both sides of the turn of the century.[10]

By the 1920s pressure against such shoots was mounting as the use of caged birds was coming to be seen as unsporting and even cruel. As a result, the Ludlow and District Gun Club was founded in 1925 for clay pigeon shooting. They had their own range on Whitcliffe that was claimed to be 'one of the best automatic clay bird ranges in the whole of England' and they certainly held national competitions attracting entrants from the length and breadth of Britain.[11]

Target shooting also became popular in the first years of the twentieth century. A rifle club was started in 1907 for both members of the new Territorial Force and former members of their forerunners, the Imperial Volunteers, as well as civilians. Both the indoor range at the Drill Hall and the outdoor range at Whitbach were used. Cup competitions were held and matches took place against similar clubs such as one at Bridgnorth. Though the club closed in 1915 as most of its members went off to war, it was revived in 1927.[12]

Target shooting as sport for all was as a result of the fear of war and of war itself. After so many volunteers, wishing to serve in the South African War at the turn of the century, were found unfit for foreign service, the government decided that Physical Education classes in schools should be overhauled. A new syllabus, based on the military training manual, was introduced and many elementary schools were issued with rifles to help in the teaching of drill.

In addition, many schools were presented with air rifles so that they could form shooting clubs. The National School on Lower Galdeford formed one and practised at their shooting range on which they held competitions. In 1907, the stationer's W H Smith and Son offered a prize of a gold nibbed fountain pen for the winner. Entrants fired from standing, kneeling and prone positions. Inter-school matches were also held.[13] As a result, as will be seen in Chapter 2, several public houses formed their own air rifle clubs in the interwar years.

Horse racing

One long-standing leisure pursuit that was still enjoyed was horse racing. It is said that the Old Field at Bromfield has seen horse racing since the mid seventeenth century, but the first official race was held in 1772 when organised flat racing was introduced. In the mid nineteenth century hurdles were added and by the 1870s a steeplechase course had been developed. The ending of racing at Bicton Heath near Shrewsbury in 1877, due to its growing reputation for 'fixed' races and the prevalence of pickpockets, helped the Ludlow races to grow in popularity. Up to the Second World War horse racing was a good example of a sport that was very exclusive in social terms, but had a huge popular following. Meets always attracted the upper classes and Ludlow races became an integral part of their

The growing popularity of a day out at Ludlow Races resulted in the opening in 1904 of a new grandstand to enable the visiting social elite, especially the ladies, a more comfortable viewing experience.

(Courtesy of Shropshire Museum Service)

With the invention of the motor car, the local gentry could travel to the local racecourse in style and use them as a viewing platform and a place to store picnics and drinks for relaxation between races.

(Courtesy of Shropshire Museum Service)

social calendar. The 1903 spring meeting saw an 'aristocratic gathering' whilst in 1905 it was reported 'in the members enclosure there was a capital muster of county gentry and hunting people from other parts of the country.' To cater for this clientele a new grandstand was opened in 1904. The races as a social event for members of the upper classes carried on and in 1921 the local press reported 'a great social gathering from the border counties' and this was typical of meetings throughout the interwar period.[14]

Before the Great War, other than the social elite, the crowd at Ludlow races tended to come from the poorer sections of the populace as the middle and lower middle-classes tended

With the opening of a railway station at Bromfield in 1852, working class spectators could now travel to the races from the industrial towns and cities of the Midlands. This photograph of a meeting in 1912 shows how popular race days were away from the enclosures and grandstand housing the upper classes. Such attendance was helped by the fact that entry for these sections of the course was free. (Courtesy of Shropshire Museum Service)

To be seen at Ludlow Races, and photographed for the family album, appears to be a must for this proud group of race goers in 1903.

(Courtesy of Shropshire Museum Service)

to keep away due to the association of race meetings with crime and general dissipation. Certainly the town magistrates' court in the days following a meeting saw a succession of drunks and pickpockets, many from outside the town, come before the bench. This especially occurred after the opening of Bromfield rail station in 1852 that allowed special race day trains to disgorge spectators from the industrial Midlands and especially Birmingham.

Attendance by the general populace was also greatly helped by the fact that until 1934 entrance to the course was free. This was due to them being subsidised by members' subscriptions and an entry charge to the stand of 12/-.[15]

LADY SYBIL LYGON AND MISS DIANA COVENTRY

LADY MARY DOYNE AND COLONEL LLOYD

MRS. BARBER STARKEY AND LADY FORESTER (right)

Well Met at Ludlow Races.

EN ROUTE FOR THE PADDOCK: MRS. ROBERT DEVEREUX AND MR. MOSS

MR. AND MRS. DOUGLAS STEWART PAUSE FOR REFLECTIONS

For the upper classes, Ludlow races was still very much part of the social calendar in the inter-war years as this photo-montage for *The Tatler* illustrates.

These Red Cross nurses were being taken to a Ludlow Race Meeting in 1922. With the influx of working class race goers from the industrial Midlands they would not only be needed to give first aid to injured jockeys but also to attend spectators who had been hurt in fights, many of which would have been fuelled by drink.
(Courtesy of Ludlow Historical Research Group [LHRG] archive)

Boisterous events: beating the bounds

As the new middle-classes took a firmer grip on power, traditional urban pursuits began to fall foul of what this new elite believed to be respectable behaviour. In Ludlow, one of the first annual events that fell victim to this new morality was the local custom of 'Processioning Day': the annual 'beating of the bounds' or walking the borough boundary. In some parishes this custom dated back before the Norman Conquest and usually occurred on Ascension Day.

In Ludlow this annual event had evolved into a mixture of piety and boisterous behaviour. Accompanied by clergymen, boys from the church schools, each carrying a birch bough, would form a procession. This started from the parish church of St Laurence and progressed to a mound near Corve Street Bridge where a cross once stood. Here an epistle was

The annual 'beating of the bounds,' led by local churchmen, had been a tradition carried on for many years. However, by the mid-nineteenth century its association and apparent encouragement of boisterous and even violent behaviour by the accompanying schoolboys, met with growing hostility. For the new middle-classes, the day's proceedings did not sit well with their newly acquired Victorian views of what constituted 'respectful' religious decorum and demeanour.

read. Going from boundary stone to boundary stone, where each one was struck using the birch boughs, the procession moved on to the Weeping Cross where the boys knelt and the gospel was read. They then wound their way along Temeside to Ludford Bridge where a decorated birch bough was fixed in the centre. The schoolboys, now using their birch boughs as weapons, would fight a pitched battle, watched and cheered on by the churchmen and the local populace, to see who could capture it. Exhausted, and with some boys no doubt bruised and bloodied, they then all walked or limped to the Guildhall in Mill Street where refreshments awaited. Though the new and growing social elite approved the religious nature of this tradition, its alliance with what they viewed as the encouragement of the acceptability of rowdy and unruly public behaviour, could not be tolerated any longer. As a result, this age-old tradition ended around 1850.[16]

Ludlow's tug of war

Yet another traditional ev men also took part.

The rules were simple. The town's population was divided into two teams: the Red team made up of residents from the Broad Street and Castle Wards and the Blue team made up of men and women from the Corve Street and Old Street Wards. The object was for a team to dip their end of the rope into the River Teme. The Broad Street and Castle Ward team had to pull it to the river at the bottom of either Mill Street or Lower Broad Street, whilst the Corve Street and Old Street Wards team had to attempt to reach the river via Old Street. It was the best of three pulls. Each time the losing team had to make a collection in order to raise the money to buy the rope off the winning team so the next pull could take place. The money was then mainly spent on drink that helped extend the day's exuberant celebrations after the contest had ended.

Waiting for the rope would be a crowd numbering about two thousand strong made up of both participants and onlookers. Respect for their 'betters' disappeared on such occasions and in 1838, when the mayor teased the crowd by delaying throwing the rope to the waiting mass, he was struck in the face by a well aimed snowball.

Other than the start and finish there were no other rules and this was to be the reason for the downfall of this age-old tradition. Violence became a feature of the day and the main attraction for the onlookers. This was a human blood sport. A journalist, reporting on the 1826 contest, recalls being:

> *'dragged into the crowd and remaining fully ten minutes borne on the shoulders of others, his feet never touching the ground and, when reaching King Street, the rope, getting round his middle, to escape being cut through, slipped it over his head and fell when hundreds trampled over him and there was no chance of rescue until the bulk of the rabble had passed, when he was removed as dead into a neighbouring shop.'*[17]

By 1839 the contest was deemed 'more violent than for many a year past, the flooring-down blows countless, (as was) the number of men and boys on their hands and knees or on their backs.'[18] Five years later a reporter again described the viciousness of the fighting.

At 4pm every Shrove Tuesday, from one of the top windows of the old Market Hall that stood in Castle Square until the mid 1880s, the Mayor would pass down a 36 yard rope to the waiting crowd. What now began was a rope-pulling contest that pitted one half of the town against the other. Mayhem was the result.

(Courtesy of Shropshire Museum Service)

'Numberless blows are dealt out on the heads and bodies of each other, many are floored, blood scatters about, hats fly in the air, shoes parting from their tenants, coats torn, men tied up in the rope and lying on the ground, trodden upon and crying for help.' [19]

Even the spectators, caught up in the excitement of cheering on their team, often resorted to fighting, much to the delight of those nearby. As was noted during one contest 'a pugilistic performance amongst the crowd, between a little crabbed looking tailor … and a huge publican six feet high and more than twenty stone, attracted great attention.'[20]

This annual event also once brought all classes of local society together for at least one day a year. This can be seen when in 1838 it was noted that the contest did not last as long as previous years. The cause was claimed to be 'owing chiefly to the smartly dressed beaux and dandies of Castle and Broad Street Wards not being disposed to a roll in the snow and mud which the streets were abundantly covered.'[21] This appears to give a clue as to the changing social nature of the contest. As the years passed, the rope pulling was being seen more and more as an occasion for the working-classes and one that was no longer fit for members of the 'respectable' classes. The county and town social worthies were now viewing it as a savage relic of the past and one that pandered to the vices of the lower orders.

'During the contest many persons were hurt and many angry blows exchanged and ended in fighting and drunkenness, which invariably follows this obsolete custom. It is high time that the authorities should put an end to the custom and that Ludlow should take her stand among her more civilised neighbours, for so long as this barbarous folly is perpetuated so long will Ludlow be considered behind in the march of civilised refinement.' [22]

This plea was repeated again two years later when it was noted that the rope pulling was:

Ludlow had its own bare-knuckle sporting hero in Robert Baldwin, born in the town in 1800, and better known as White Headed Bob. In May 1828 he fought Ned Neale at Ascot Heath near Windsor for a purse of £250. The fight was forcibly stopped after 80 rounds when a local magistrate forced his way through the crowd to halt the contest on grounds of public safety.
(Courtesy of Albion Prints)

'attended with the usual fighting and drunkenness among the lower part of the inhabitants. It is time this foolish and barbarous practice was done away with but it is feared it will not be until someone is killed.'[23]

This prophecy was not fulfilled as at last Ludlow's leaders acted and banned any further contests. 1853 had seen the last of them. Victorian respectability had won the day.

Bare-knuckle fighting

Another victim of the new moral compass was bare-knuckle or prize fighting. At the beginning of the nineteenth century this sport was popular with all classes both as participants as well as spectators. The Reverend Baugh (Rector of St Laurence 1803-1837) was a proponent who challenged and fought the Rector Green of Burfield to see who was the best man.[24] A prizefight in Ludford Park in 1829 attracted hundreds of spectators that encompassed the full spectrum of social class. They turned up from far and wide both in personal carriages and on foot. Local innkeepers had put up a purse of £100 to attract the two most famous fighters of the day to travel to Ludlow. Young Dutch Sam stayed at the *Clive Arms* at Bromfield whilst Ned Neale took accommodation at the *Angel Hotel* on Broad Street.

In a fight that excited national interest, Dutch Sam won with a blow to the throat of his opponent after 78 rounds lasting a total of one hour 41 minutes.[25]

As the years passed, however, the town's growing Victorian middle-class, with their new moralistic outlook, began to frown upon such contests especially when organised by the local working-class. In 1864, when Charles Owen, a nail maker from Riverside, fought Caleb Spear, a painter from Lower Galdeford, both fighters found themselves in court. Frustratingly for the magistrates, as bare-knuckle fighting was still legal the two could only be charged with causing a

Before the First Word War bare-knuckle fighting was still quite widespread amongst the working classes both in Ludlow and the surrounding villages. In this photograph, taken in Cornbrook, Clee Hill c1914 three neighbouring families, the Tennants, the Wiltshires and the Hopewells, look on as two of their younger family members strike a pose. (Courtesy of Ancestry Website)

Ludford Park in 1829 was the setting for one of the biggest bare-knuckle fights of that year between Dutch Sam and Ned Neale. Local innkeepers who had put up a £100 purse for the winner had lured them to Ludlow. This epic fight of 78 rounds made front-page news in sporting circles.

breach of the peace.[26] A court case of 1882 proved a turning point. This decided that a bare-knuckle fight was an assault occasioning actual bodily harm, even though the participants had consented. Though this left the sport in a grey legal area, as it had still not been banned by parliamentary legislation, it marked the end of widespread contests in England though such fights did carry on.

A Ludlow resident, interviewed in 1929, recalled that a number of fights for a purse were still being organised in the town in the late 19th century. Illegal widespread side bets were also the norm. Though on the wane, such fights still occurred in the 1920s. James Charmer, an ex-miner who returned to Ludlow after the Great War, took part in a number of them.[27]

Guy Fawkes day

Another annual event in the popular calendar came under the same growing social pressures to change. This was Guy Fawkes Day that celebrated the frustrating of a Roman Catholic plot of 1605 to assassinate the King and members of the House of Lords and Commons. An Act of Parliament in 1606 made the day an annual public day of thanksgiving. Young men of both the labouring and shopkeeping classes, sometimes aided by the sons of the higher social orders, took part in the local celebrations. A large bonfire was constructed and effigies were made. These were often paraded through the streets before being thrown on the fire, sometimes after a mock trial. For many years these events were supported through patronage by the middle and upper classes who saw the day as a celebration of 'English Liberty,' 'English Institutions' and the death of 'Foreign Catholicism,' whist the lower middle-classes viewed it in terms of popular Protestantism. As the years progressed, the labouring classes began to see the day as a time of raucous merriment and a way of showing their displeasure through the burning of effigies, not only of Guy Fawkes, but also of local dignitaries who had offended them in some way.

As the nineteenth century progressed, the ever-growing, respectable middle-classes started to suppress such behaviour, as the protection of property and control of law and order in public places became a vital part of the values held by Victorian authorities. In many isolated rural areas such as South Shropshire, away from the growth of industrialisation and modernisation, Guy Fawkes celebrations still managed to be carried on virtually unaltered but the tide of change was inevitable. In 1859 the 'Thanksgiving Act' of 1606 was finally repealed but the first move against these traditional celebrations occurred a few years earlier in Ludlow.

It began in 1847. It had been the custom, started by the Municipal Corporation, and then taken over by the Ludlow Borough Council when it was formed in 1836, that the townsfolk would be given a cart loaded with coal with which to make a fire in Castle Square. This originally had been introduced to stop the damage to gates, fences, hedges and trees in the search for wood to burn. This annual gift to the populace was ended and the immediate result was public disorder.

At 5 o'clock on Guy Fawkes Day the young men of the town, feeling betrayed, went on the rampage as a search was made to find fuel with which to build a fire. They cut down trees on Castle Walk and on Whitcliffe, removed gates, pulled down fences and even stripped a barn owned by the mayor. At

In the nineteenth century November 5th would see a torchlight procession wend its way through the streets of Ludlow with young men carrying an effigy of Guy Fawkes preceded by a fife and drum band. They would then cross Ludford Bridge to the Whitcliffe where, after a mock trial, he would be consigned to the flames. On occasions effigies of unpopular local figures would join Guy Fawkes.

9.30pm, as the bonfire was lit, the police intervened to stop further wood being collected.

The populace met this with force and a fight broke out and the son of the publican of the *Sun Inn* was hit on the head by a police truncheon and seriously hurt. The crowd were only just persuaded by the young man's father not to throw the guilty policeman on the bonfire. To make the town authorities aware of their anger, the youth of Ludlow now paraded the streets, headed by one of them using a tin kettle as a drum whilst two of his friends accompanied him playing fifes.[28]

The result of that night's events was that the ritual lighting of the town's bonfire, instead of being ended, merely moved. As one spectator later noted, though bonfires could be seen 'in several parts of the town and neighbourhood … Whitcliffe Hill was the centre place of attraction, being literally covered with bonfires large and small. Bonfires were also lit at the Grammar School, the Workhouse etc. (with) the usual accompaniment of rockets, squibs, crackers, fire balls etc.'[29]

Though Castle Square no longer saw a bonfire, the organised celebration of November 5th still started in the centre of the town. Over one hundred young men, carrying an effigy of Guy Fawkes sitting on a barrel and carrying a lantern, led a torchlight procession. They paraded through the streets, lined with cheering crowds, setting off fireworks incessantly. They would then cross Ludford Bridge and head to Whitcliffe where a mock trial was held before consigning Guy Fawkes to the bonfire. An attempt by the local authorities to curb this new yet still raucous tradition was made in 1879.

The police were instructed by the borough council not only to stop the annual torchlight procession through the streets but also the letting off of fireworks along the way. They insisted that all such celebrations should take place outside the borough boundary. Realising that trouble might flare up due to this order, the local constabulary were reinforced for the day by the Herefordshire force. However, they were not

The original maypole was a tall birch pole, possibly painted or decorated with flowers, that was a focal point for dancing, drinking and general merrymaking. By the twentieth century, as this photograph from 1934 shows, May Day celebrations had been sanitised and now consisted of young children dancing in circles whilst holding coloured ribbons attached to the top of the pole.
(Courtesy of LHRG Archive)

needed, but the ban was still soon lifted as the people chose a different tactic to fight it. The effigies now being burnt on Whitcliffe each year not only represented Guy Fawkes but also unpopular local figures such as the councillors and churchmen who had instigated the ban. Faced with this very public show of personal hostility the ban was quietly forgotten.

As the century progressed the effigies carried in the main procession now became national hate figures rather than local ones. In 1899, during the South African War, they were of Boer Commanders. In 1904 the effigies were of the Russian Ambassador and his wife. Some effigies remained local, especially in smaller private processions. Annie Nicholas of Corve Street and Harriet Didlick of the Brickyard paraded caricatures of Richard Adlington, a local wheelwright, and his wife. This was part of a fifteen-year-old personal feud.

The May Fair was also a time when stallholders displayed their wares along the High Street. Here could be purchased trinkets of all kinds along with exotic fruits and confectionery treats. For farm and domestic servants who were paid just twice a year, one of them being May Day, the temptation to spend some of it on such luxuries was great. (Courtesy of Ludlow Museum Service)

When police blocked their way they turned into a nearby field and set fire to the effigies there.[30] An eyewitness account of a bonfire night procession in 1895 is given by Arthur Everall in his recollections of his early childhood whilst living at the top of Corve Street.

> *'There was a great torchlight procession preceded by a drum and fife band, followed by effigies of unpopular public and local celebrities. The rear was escorted by a number of young farmers on horseback. This procession proceeded up Corve Street, past our house, through the town to the Whitcliff (sic), where the effigy were duly consigned to the flames of a huge bonfire, to the accompaniment of fireworks and appropriate music.'*[31]

But animosity from the authorities slowly began to have an effect. November 5th celebrations began to wane as the idea as to what constituted 'respectable' behaviour permeated down to the lower middle-classes. As their support diminished and was finally lost so was most of the organising force. From 1905 the planning of the evening's proceedings was now being left to individual public houses. In that year the parade started at the *Portcullis Inn* on Upper Galdeford and after passing through the streets of Ludlow ended on the Smithfield where a bonfire was lit. The next year it was the turn of the *Eagle and Child* on Corve Street. By 1911 even these shortened festivities had ended and Guy Fawkes Night was becoming a domestic affair with most bonfires only being lit in gardens and celebrated by families or groups of friends and neighbours. Another traditional, boisterous celebration of the people had been tamed.[32]

Christmas and New Year celebrations

Even Christmas celebrations began to fall foul of small town respectability. Yuletide Waits were a long-standing tradition. Until 1835 the town had sponsored groups of musicians to wake households on Christmas morning. This was based on 'watch night' or waitnight' as shepherds once did on Christmas Eve. Once the sponsorship ended this evolved into small groups of musicians, or even bands, playing seasonal tunes throughout the entire Christmas period. Joining them would be carol singers. A few of these were church and chapel-goers raising funds for various good causes. However, many were made up of seasonally unemployed men taking the opportunity of collecting money to help themselves and their families. In addition, children joined in, knocking on doors of the more wealthy classes asking for Christmas gifts often 'to the great annoyance of the servant maids who had to answer so frequently to the loud and oft-repeated taps at the door.'[33]

By the turn of the twentieth century the door-to-door visits by children were being seen as 'only an excuse for

As the years passed the proceedings grew more secular. By 1914 it was the Town Band who entertained the New Year revellers who would congregate at the Buttercross whilst popular songs were sung both before and after *Auld Lang Syne*. By the 1920s, a few churches and chapels still held watch nights, whilst the bulk of the people would entertain themselves at the top of Broad Street, in front of the Buttercross, dancing to the tunes played by ukulele and banjo players.[37]

Maypole dancing and the May Fair

The rites of welcoming springtime fertility also came under moral scrutiny. Dating back to pagan times, a tall birch pole was erected on May Day, sometimes painted or decorated with flowers, around which the populace danced to welcome in

In addition to local church and chapel groups singing carols throughout the streets of the town, there were also bands of seasonally unemployed men, with varied musical skills, going from door to door in the hope of being given cash gifts or even gifts in kind. Such men were still to be seen and heard during the festive weeks of the interwar years.

Spring. Drink was also an important aspect of the enjoyment and added to the boisterous nature of the celebration. It was usual for farm labourers to be given the day off work to attend, though in the towns, where the new habit of set working hours ushered in by the Industrial Revolution held good, employers were not so amenable. As a result the last communal maypole in Ludlow was erected in Old Street in 1864 but this had rotted away by 1876. A local landlord now took the celebrations under his wing and a maypole could now be found behind the *Horse and Jockey* public house on Holdgate Fee. For a number of years, on May Day, dancers would cavort to the sound of fiddles, often commandeering the street as part of their dance floor.[38]

One way the middle-classes curbed this annual celebration was to encourage the attaching of ribbons to the maypole. Men and women would now take part in a disciplined dance in pairs, men going one way and women the other so that ribbons would intertwine until the pole was enveloped and the dancers came together at its foot. Increasingly the dancers became boys and girls and this was seen in Ludlow when, as part of the annual Charities Parade in 1907, the pupils of Brimfield School gave an exhibition of plaiting the maypole. This was seen again in 1923 as part of a pageant held on the Castle Green. Boys and girls from each school in Ludlow gave an exhibition of choreographed maypole dancing.[39] Yet another working-class day of exuberance had been tamed.

At the same time of year the annual May Fair was held. This was traditionally a hiring fair for both domestic and farm servants but mainly the latter. As the nineteenth century progressed it remained a hiring fair. As a writer explained in 1845, this was the one time when 'the servants, both male and female, are in the habit of changing their places and all looking forward to fresh hiring and consequent increases in wages.' It appears that it was traditional that waggoners looking for employment would signal their skill by wearing a length of whipcord in their hats. Similarly, cowmen would display a tuft of cow hair, shepherds a ball of wool, whilst dairymaids wore a clean white apron and white cotton socks. When a negotiation was successfully agreed the new employee would be given a shilling by the hirer that would bind them for the next twelve months. However, by 1881 it was claimed that 'very little hiring (was) done, most of those present being on pleasure bent.'[40] It was no longer just a day when young men and women searched for fresh employment but also, since they were paid six monthly, it was a time for enjoyment and fraternisation whilst they had the jingle of coins about them.

Once mainly a hiring fair, by 1906 Ludlow's May Fair had become overwhelmingly a pleasure fair. Brightly lit by electricity, exciting rides and thrills of all kinds were on offer and looked forward to by most of the populace, especially the working-classes.
(Courtesy of Shropshire Museum Service)

The May Fair was a time when crowds descended on the centre of Ludlow from far and wide. Not only were exciting rides to be had but, as the boy in the centre shows, it was also a time to enjoy gastronomic treats. (Courtesy of Shropshire Museum Service)

The May Fair had become:

'The day which, above all others in the year, is devoted to fun and frolic and on which we expect to see the greatest number of healthy lads and bonny lasses congregated in the ancient borough' whilst the bells of St Laurence 'rang merrily throughout all the day.' [41]

A typical scene was described thus:

'About 2 o'clock the country lads and lassies began to make their appearance in their holiday hose, as gay as butterflies, gazing with delight and wonder at the different shows that were in attendance.' [42]

At the 1866 fair could be found shooting galleries, photograph booths, collections of wild beasts and reptiles, waxworks, boxing booths, a hobby horse roundabout and freak shows such as the human skeleton, the fat lady and the dwarf as well as a 'so-called Caffre (African) who devoured rats and rabbits apparently with as much gusto as a schoolboy

When the circus came to town it first paraded around the streets to advertise itself to the populace and often stayed in Castle Square for a while to allow crowds to see the attractions offered. This parade from the 1890s is probably on its way to the Smithfield off Lower Galdeford where most circus big tops were erected. (Shropshire Museum Services)

would eat plum pudding.' In addition, could be found the temptations of an 'immense quantity of trinkets, gingerbreads, oranges, nuts and sugar cane on the stalls which bordered both sides of Castle Street and Mill Street as far as the Guildhall.'[43]

As the years passed the fair's attractions grew. By the Edwardian years the patrons could experience racing cars, steam yachts and merry-go-rounds though the main attraction was then the new cinematograph where large queues constantly formed. Added to this, all was now illuminated by electric light at a time when most would go home to a single gaslight and even candles.[44]

As could be expected the day had its rowdy, raucous and even criminal side. 'Even before dusk, vigorous dances could be seen through the open windows of the public houses' and 'as usual, several persons were brought up the day after the fair charged with being drunk, pocket picking etc.'[45] The result was that the town's 'respectable' elders began to try to restrict what they saw as growing public disorder, fuelled by drink which encouraged sins of the flesh and criminality.

In 1870 the town council refused to allow any show folk to enter the town to set up their rides and stalls until after 8pm on the Sunday evening after all religious services had ended. This ploy failed and merely resulted in the fair setting up on the Saturday on land just a few yards outside the borough boundary near Corve Bridge. The council's second attempt to obstruct the popularity of the fair and curb the behaviour of the visiting crowds, was to limit the opening hours of the public houses to just 1-4pm. As was pointed out at the time, this meant that fairgoers would have to consume all of their drink in a short space of time rather than spreading the consumption out throughout the day. This sowed 'grave doubts in the minds of many whether [this is more] likely to encourage rather than diminish the evils which it was intended to prevent.'[46] This proved to be true and both edicts were removed in the following years.

The churches too tried to alter the way that the fairgoers enjoyed themselves. Groups of churchgoers took stalls at the fair to distribute and sell religious tracts. In addition they sang hymns and preached to the crowd regarding the sins of their 'enjoyment.' This intervention also met criticism in that it was pointed out that this could just make the situation worse. As a local editorial explained:

> *'We give the caterers of such things all credit for their good intentions but we think that their presence brings religion into contempt and is the cause of many unpleasant remarks. That a great deal of evil is present we doubt not, but another time and place is preferable to the decrying of it. People go out for fun and fun they will have somehow and it seems a pity that innocently conceived enjoyments should be interlarded by so-called religionists.'*[47]

There were also unsuccessful calls to move the fair. Councillor Henry Weyman, a local solicitor who lived at the top of Mill Street, complained of the noise of the fair and the 'great amount of drunkenness and other forms of vice' that accompanied it. He believed that if it could not be stopped then at least it should be moved away from the centre of the town where so many respectable people lived. Weyman wanted it moved to the Smithfield, nearer to the working-class part of the town.[48] Despite all these pressures, the May Fair survived in its traditional setting.

The travelling circus

One relatively new tradition by 1850 was the annual visit by a circus. After the travelling circus tent was introduced to the United Kingdom in 1836, the circus, originally static in a few towns and cities, was freed to travel the length and breadth of the country and be introduced to new audiences. Those that came to Ludlow at first utilised various sites before settling on the Jockey Field off Old Street and the Smithfield. As well as portraying equestrian skills, acrobats and clowns, audiences were offered the chance to experience the sight of dangerous wild animals such as lions and tigers. The excitement and wonder that this generated, at a time when the horizons of most of those watching were limited to just Ludlow and the surrounding area, can only be imagined. The initial parade through the town when the circus first arrived was the first treat.

Typical of this was the arrival of Lord Sanger's Circus throughout the 1890s. There would be a Grand Procession led by elephants and camels followed by over twenty carriages containing wild beasts such as lions, tigers, leopards, wolves, bears and crocodiles. In addition, other carriages would offer onlookers various exotic tableaux. Such events also offered the chance of vicarious danger. In 1896 a lion escaped its cage and had to be hunted down and shot near Ashford Hall, whilst in 1906 as an elephant walked down Bell Lane it stood on the wooden cover to the cellar of No.18 splintering it and causing the elephant to collide with the house wall. This led to a 'general stampede of onlookers.'[49]

Other excitements were more organised. In 1875 one of the clowns from Ginnet's Circus performed aquatic feats in the river near Ludford Bridge before each performance, whilst in 1894 Lord Sanger's Circus on the Smithfield put on two performances of a re-enactment of the war in the Sudan. This was billed as showing warfare on the banks of the Nile with 1,500 soldiers, Arabs and Red Cross nurses along with 250 horses, camels and elephants plus cannons. It was claimed that 7,000 people could view the spectacle over two performances. In 1901 the show was changed to a mock South African War battle with 'hundreds of men, hundreds of horses, real Boers, Swazis, Matabeles and camp followers.'[50]

When a circus visited, elephants, camels and other exotic animals were paraded to delight and excite the watching crowds. Many of these animals, to amaze the paying customers, could be seen in spectacles of military re-enactments with a cast of hundreds such as imagined battles along the banks of the River Nile.
(Shropshire Museum Service)

Unlike the May Fair these annual mass entertainments came under no threat from the authorities. This was partly because they were not held in places surrounded by public houses, partly because all classes enjoyed them and partly because the entrance fees that varied from just 6d to 10/6d (over half of a farmworker's weekly wage) ensured social segregation.

Winter celebrations: ice and snow

A few traditional pastimes survived. As long as their boisterous nature was kept within respectable bounds they were tolerated. It helped especially if those taking part came from all classes. Winter pursuits such as ice skating and tobogganing fell into this category. Winters in the nineteenth and early twentieth century were far colder than now. The River Teme often iced over during the winter months, especially the deep waters near the castle, as did the River Corve. When this occurred the town came out to play. Men, women, boys and girls from all social classes congregated on the ice to skate and impromptu games of ice hockey with homemade sticks were played. People without skates could hire them for the day or just slide using their own everyday footwear.

The enterprising landlord of the *Imperial Vaults* at the top of Old Street even organised an ice carnival in 1895. Over six hundred people turned up to skate or cavort on the ice whilst numerous others watched from the Castle Walks. Lamps and torches lit the whole event whilst a band played music to allow couples to dance the night away. When possible, skating also took place on the large pool in Oakley Park with large crowds often in attendance. Many from the town would also make their way out to the frozen pool at Ledwyche where an enterprising farmer charged 6d to skate in the afternoon and 3d in the evening, all proceeds being donated to Shrewsbury Infirmary. Though cold winters grew less common, skating could still occur at the pool as in 1928 and 1933, though by then it was possible to skate further into the night, courtesy of car headlights.[51]

Tobogganing was also a popular annual pastime during the winter months. When snow fell, the youth of the town were to be seen journeying to Whitcliffe with their mainly homemade toboggans.

> *'Youths, maidens and children were to be seen trooping up with their sleighs. There was a nice run on Wednesday on top of the*

Not everyone had ice skates so enterprising shopkeepers hired them out to would be skaters so that the thrill of being on the frozen river could be enjoyed more fully. The lady on the right is having such a pair fitted. Some young men, as can be seen, came with homemade ice hockey sticks to enjoy an impromptu game.

hill, but the greater part of the sport took place in the dingle, where dozens of parties kept descending and ascending.'

All were watched by snowball-hurling spectators who gave roars of laughter when anyone came to grief.[52] The same winter scene of enjoyment could be seen throughout the interwar years when 'practically all the younger and many

of the older generation of the town visited the hill for the exhilarating sport of tobogganing.'

As well as tobogganing down from the top of Whitcliffe, many made use of the road from the *Bowling Green Inn* to the *Charlton Arms Hotel* until the police finally stopped them. Three young men who later found themselves in court, claimed in their defence that the road had been used for such

At the turn of the twentieth century the River Teme often froze over and then people of all ages and classes came out to enjoy the experience of standing on the frozen waters.

a purpose for many years and no one had ever been stopped before. Such winter enjoyments within the town, however, had been discouraged for a number of years. In 1914 six boys from Lower Galdeford, who had made ice slides on the road outside their homes, found themselves in the Magistrates Court being fined 1/- each. As traffic increased there was a limit as to what the authorities would tolerate.[53]

By 1914, though a few traditional leisure pursuits had survived, and some had even prospered, a number of mainly urban leisure pursuits had been curtailed and many ended by the ruling, 'respectable' elites. However, for generations the focal point of everyday leisure for many of the working-classes had been the public house. As the next chapter will show, this too was coming under pressure to change.

CHAPTER 2

The War against the Public House

In 1850 there were 71 public houses in Ludlow, one for every 72 people in the borough, and they were the hub of working class leisure activity. It was in such places that many of the 'respectable classes' felt that many of the lower orders spent money that should have been saved in order to better themselves or to provide for their families. Over the years these 'high-minded' people would put great effort into a struggle to weaken what they saw as the detrimental grip that the public house had on much of the populace.

So what were these places like inside and who exactly were their patrons? Ludlow's public houses came in all shapes and sizes, having different numbers of rooms, many quite small, with different names attached to them. There could be a taproom where beer brewed on the premises was tapped straight from the source. Then there could be a bar where, in addition to beer, wines and spirits could be had. Drinks would be a little cheaper there than in the slightly more comfortably

It is perhaps understandable why many labouring men frequented the public houses so often when their home situation is taken into account. Most working-class homes in Ludlow consisted of only one room on the ground floor though a few had a small scullery attached. In this one main room the entire family lived their daily lives. This meant husband, wife and children, plus sometimes members of the extended family, would all congregate in the same cramped space lit at night by just a single gas lamp. In this one room all the cooking took place, all meals were eaten, and on wet days all washing was dried. In addition, baths would be taken in front of the fire at weekends. The joy of an escape to a warm, well-lit

Singing was often heard in public. May Bradley, née Smith, of Romany descent, seen here with her husband Thomas outside their house in Old Street in 1964, was famous for her voice especially in her younger days. May often sang Romany songs in her local the *Hen and Chickens* as well as other public houses throughout the town. Her reward would be in the form of drinks. (Courtesy of Rob Bradley)

environment, where a drink could be taken with friends and a pub game played, can be better understood today, though at the time one town councillor showed his ignorance of the realities of working-class home life when he partly placed the blame on the shoulders of some wives. He claimed that:

'Many a man after he was married discovered that his wife did not know her domestic duties and could not make a comfortable home. The result was that the man went to the public house where he found some degree of comfort.'[2]

But all customers were not male. It is estimated that women made up 25-30% of the Ludlow clientele, about the same proportion as those charged with drunkenness in the local Magistrates Court. The women drinking midweek tended to belong to the lower working-class, whilst at weekends the wives of the lower middle-class and skilled working-class visited with their husbands. In Ludlow, with its many market days, farmers' wives could often be found in the public houses being served with both food and drink. On some days over forty of them could be found in the *Grape Vaults* on Old Street, though they tended to congregate in a separate room to the male customers. This can be seen when the landlord of the *Golden Lion* on Old Street asked for permission to make a separate outside door into the smoke room that was situated behind the bar. This was 'because on market days farmer's wives had to come right through the bar to this room where they waited for their husbands.'[3]

Prostitution and brothels

Younger and especially single women tended to stay away from public houses as they did not want to be seen in the same light as the prostitutes who often frequented them looking for custom. When the police were objecting to the renewal of the licence of the *Grape Vaults* on Old Street, it was claimed that on a Saturday night there could be found on the premises a number of women not having refreshments: almost certainly a euphemism for prostitutes.

Measuring the number of prostitutes in Ludlow at any one time is very difficult but it appears their number was relatively large. The police charge books for the period 1865-1882 still survive though the detail they give varies greatly. More often than not, the occupations of the people charged is not listed nor their full addresses, just the charge and any subsequent action or sentence. However, occasionally, when a woman is a known prostitute, even if the charge is drunkenness, assault, abusive language or even theft, this has sometimes been noted. In this way 61 women can be identified as prostitutes though this number is certainly a gross under-estimation. In addition, the *Blue Book of Judicial Statistics* for the county in 1865 lists eight brothels in the town. From the named brothel keepers charged, it can be ascertained that a brothel in Ludlow usually comprised two or three young women living in a property that was looked after by a mature brothel keeper, usually a woman. Most also appear to be situated in the Upper and Lower Galdeford area.[4]

It may appear strange to include prostitution as a leisure activity but, according to the police charge books, those availing themselves of the services of such women were mainly from the surrounding villages: farmers, farm labourers and waggoners. Many such men, visiting Ludlow for the numerous fairs, auctions and markets, looked forward to such encounters. For a short time they would be in the company of strangers and away from the watchful gaze of wives and girlfriends or the prying, all-seeing eyes of fellow villagers.

Music and song in Ludlow public houses

But whatever the reason for visiting public houses, they were places where entertainment in a number of forms was provided, alongside the drink. Music and singing often abounded. Talented, and at times not so talented, customers would serenade their fellow drinkers. John Fury played his banjo in the *Pheasant Inn* on the corner of Tower Street and

Old Street, whilst his friend accompanied him on the flute. It was while singing was being enjoyed at the *Half Moon* public house on Lower Galdeford that a fight broke out when a group's loud conversation hindered others from listening. At the *Fox Inn* on Upper Galdeford a Coroner's Court was told that customers were so engrossed in enjoying the evening's singing that they failed to notice that one of their number had been dead in his seat for some time.[5] By the interwar years most public houses boasted a piano. In 1934, when members of the Ludlow Boxing Club held their first annual dinner at the *Queen's Head* at Galdeford, a number of them gathered around the piano and, as the pianist played popular tunes, all joined

By the 1930s darts had become the most popular game played in the town's public houses and in 1938 the first town darts league was formed with an initial ten teams joining. Darts was also very popular in the surrounding villages and this photograph from 1938 is of the prize-winning team from the Victoria Inn, Clee Hill.
(Courtesy of Paula Walker)

in the singing.[6] One young lady, who returned, aged twenty, to Ludlow in 1940, recalled that there was always music to be heard in most of the town's public houses. Someone would start playing the piano or some other instrument, such as the harmonica or ukulele, and the customers would then have a good singsong.[7] The daughter of the landlord of the *Hen and Chickens* on Old Street recalls that they had a piano in the back room and one regular often brought in his accordion. As a result, singing could be heard on most nights.[8]

Not only did customers listen and sing to the music, they also danced to it. This was widespread on nights such as New Year's Eve or during the May Fair, but also was common on numerous other occasions throughout the year especially at weekends when more women visited public houses. The type of dancing usually witnessed was known as step dancing. This was when the upper body often remained still and most of the movement was from the waist down usually with intricate foot movements. Men and women often could be seen dancing on their own or sometimes in twos or small groups. Touching a partner whilst dancing was rarely seen. In the interwar years, James Charmer often danced on tables to entertain fellow public house customers and when his relatives visited from Lancashire they would give exhibitions of clog dancing.[9]

Pub sports and games

Patrons could also take part in various pub sports and games. In the early and mid nineteenth century, as we saw in Chapter 1, a few were urban blood sports such as cockfighting. Others were more ad hoc such as in 1849 when 98 rats were released on the floor of an unnamed local inn to be killed by dogs.[10]

Puff and dart was an early form of darts that was played widely throughout Shropshire and Herefordshire in the late nineteenth century. Court cases for drunkenness and fighting mention the game quite frequently. Small homemade darts, often constructed from pieces of worsted and a pin, were puffed

Outdoor quoits could only be played at public houses that had enough suitable space near at hand. In Ludlow it tended to be played by middle-class men who could afford the metal quoits and also the means to travel to play teams often some miles from the town. Working class men tended to play the indoor variety with a target table usually found under the dartboard. This team was photographed behind the *Queen's Head Hotel* at the town end of Lower Galdeford. (Courtesy of Shropshire Museum Service)

through a tube at a target. This would often be three or four concentric circles drawn on a piece of paper fixed to a wall. Accidents could and did happen. When drawing breath before blowing at the target the dart could be inadvertently sucked down the throat requiring emergency treatment by a doctor or on occasions causing a fatality.[11] The game in this form had all but disappeared by 1914, being replaced by a wooden 'French dart' that was now thrown at the target.

In the 1920s brass barrels with cane shafts and feather and paper flights were slowly introduced. The target too evolved and the present dartboard divided into twenty numbers became standardised. By the 1930s darts had become the most widespread of pub games although it was not until 1938 that a Ludlow Darts League was formed at a meeting at the *Star and Garter* on Corve Street. The other teams in that first year's league were the *Queen's Head, Unicorn, Compasses, Bull Ring Tavern, New Inn, Portcullis, Charlton Arms, Nelson* and the *Smithfield*. Each team had eleven players and each player played one individual game. The winning team was the one that won at least six of the games.[12] Though the Second World War intervened, by 1946 eighteen public houses now had a team. Two leagues of nine were formed and the winners of each met in a Grand Final.[13]

Bagatelle, an early forerunner of bar billiards, was also popular although, because it required a seven-foot-long playing table, it tended to be found just in the larger public houses. The *George Hotel* on Castle Street had a separate bagatelle room, whilst the landlord of the *Golden Lion* on Old Street even organised an away match for his customers at the *Ship Inn* at Tenbury with a return fixture. The game also crossed the social boundaries with a table to be found at the Conservative Club.

The game survived well into the twentieth century with a league being formed in the 1920s that included teams from the *Horse and Jockey* and the *Green Dragon* on Old Street, the *Eagle Vaults*, the *Trotting Horse* and the *Compasses* on Corve Street, the *Portcullis* on Upper Galdeford, the *Half Moon* and the *Smithfield* on Lower Galdeford and the *Barley Mow* on Lower Broad Street.[14]

Skittles was another game played locally. This was not table skittles but a game played on full-sized skittle alleys with full-sized wooden pins and large wooden balls. Because of the space required there were only a few places to play the game. There were alleys at the *Ludlow Arms* on Whitcliffe and at the *Charlton Arms* at Ludford Bridge whilst one could also be found at the *Portcullis Inn* on Upper Galdeford constructed at the back of the property.

As can be seen it was mainly the middle-classes who played billiards and tables could be found at the Conservative and Liberal Clubs as well as at the town's main hotels such as the *Feathers* and the *Bull* on the Bull Ring or the larger and more respectable public houses. (Courtesy of Shropshire Museum Service)

As for other pub games, draughts, dominoes and ringboard were also very popular. The latter game was played by throwing rubber rings to land over numbered hooks on a shield-shaped wooden board fixed to a wall.[15] Quoits was another popular pastime. The outdoor version could only be played when space was available and was to be seen at the *Nelson Inn* at Rocks Green, the *Queen's Head* on Upper Galdeford and behind the *Charlton Arms Hotel*. The pitch was probably eighteen yards long with a three-foot square clay bed at both ends, encased in a wooden frame, with a centrally-placed pin. Clay was used so that a quoit could embed itself if necessary. This was another game that crossed social barriers though the town team that played on land near to the Corve Bridge tended not to be comprised of working-class men. This can be seen when by 1893 they had moved to the *Charlton Arms Hotel*, and

Roland Venables, a barrister from Richards Castle, presented the club with two pairs of metal quoits. The chairman of the club was Councillor Lear, a grocer, and the secretary was Philip Pepler, the school attendance officer. By now matches were being played against teams from as far away as Hereford, Cheltenham and Worcester and funds were required to cover travel costs that many could not afford.[16]

For most working-class adherents of the game a number of public houses allowed an indoor version to be played using rope or rubber rings and it was still being played widely in 1950. The same space used for playing darts was utilised. Often, under the dartboard, could be found a table on which a stone

The *Charlton Arms Hotel*, next to Ludford Bridge, was alone in offering its patrons clock golf. This photograph, taken just before the First World War, shows two clocks that had the twelve numbers marked. Participants would putt from each number in turn and the number of strokes taken totalled to find a winner.
(Courtesy of Graham (Floyd) Wilson-Lloyd)

or marble square slab was laid. Around a central upright peg, two concentric circles were marked: one of 8 inches in diameter and one of 12 inches. When not in use, to safeguard the playing surface from falling darts, it was protected by a piece of wood with a central hole to accommodate the peg. Two oches, or throwing marks, one for darts and the other for quoits, the latter usually being 10 ft away, were marked on the floor.

The rules being played in Ludlow in the interwar years are to be found in a report of a match played at the *Borough Arms* on Raven Lane against the *Raven Inn*. Each team had eleven members and each player played another individual, the winner being the first to reach exactly 61 points. Five points were scored for ringing the peg, three points for landing exactly within the inner circle and one point for being exactly within the outer circle. The overall winner of the match was not the most individual games won but the team with the highest accrued point score.[17]

Another game widely played in Ludlow's public houses for many years, and still popular in 1950, was Tippits. Two teams of three, with the captain in the middle, would face each other over a table. The starting team would place all their hands under the table and the captain would press a small object, usually a coin, into one of the hands. At a given command all clenched hands would be placed on the table. The opposing team, who were allowed to confer, had to decide which hand held the coin and, when chosen, tapped or tipped the hand. If the guess was wrong the team hiding the coin scored and then hid the coin again. If, however, the guess was correct the control of hiding of the coin was passed over to that team.

A few public houses also offered miniature shooting ranges. The *Greyhound Inn* on Upper Galdeford boasted a small range where air gun shooting took place and contests held against visiting teams. A miniature rifle range could also be found behind the *Hop Pole Inn* on Mill Street. At a competition held there in 1906, 17 men entered, many of them members of the local Volunteer Force, the forerunner of the Territorials.[18] In 1926 the *Raven Inn*, at the top of New Street, opened an air gun range and invited the mayor, Alderman John Palmer, to fire the first shot. It was hoped to set up an Air Gun Club in Ludlow and to have an Air Gun League. The *Eagle Vaults* on Corve Street soon joined them.[19]

Billiards was also on offer to patrons at 'respectable' hotels and public houses. From 1890 the Imperial Wine and Spirit Vaults at the top of Old Street held an annual billiards handicap. At the first event, the three prizes were a silver mounted dressing case, silver mounted carvers and a morocco cigar case, emphasising the social station of the competitors. As well as being housed at the local Conservative and Liberal Clubs, billiard rooms could be found at the *Ludlow Arms* on Whitcliffe, the *Charlton Arms* at Ludford Bridge, the *Blue Boar* on Mill Street, the *Bull* and *Feathers Hotels* on the Bull Ring and the *Queen's Head* at Galdeford.[20]

Smoking concerts were another favourite social activity offered at a number of hostelries. They too tended to cater for the middle or lower middle-class clientele though not exclusively; it depended on the organisers. Those at the *Feathers Hotel* or the *Bull Hotel* tended to be enjoyed by middle-class men. On such evenings they would entertain themselves with singing, both solos and duets, a number of comic recitations, and also instrumental numbers. At the *Greyhound Inn* or the *Blue Boar* on Mill Street, the guests would be slightly lower on the social scale but the type of entertainment would be basically the same. The *Portcullis Inn* on Upper Galdeford held such events every few weeks, as they were so popular. In 1899, a gramophone, the new 'talking machine' was the star attraction.[21]

Other public houses put on special events for their patrons. The *Nelson* at Rocks Green held pony races and athletic sports in an adjacent field, whilst the landlord of the *Hen and Chickens* on Holdgate Fee also organised foot races for prizes in an adjoining field. This would then be followed by an evening of open-air dancing. The *Charlton Arms Hotel* in 1911 even offered professional outdoor entertainment, inviting a travelling company to it as a venue offering shows twice daily at 2.30 and 7.30pm.

'The Jesters have an excellent pitch in the grounds of the *Charlton Arms Hotel*, the ground rising in terraces and the stage being raised and nicely lighted.'[22]

When not being used as an outside theatre venue, this space was being utilised for hotel's customers to enjoy a game of clock golf. Staying guests could also enjoy free fishing. Some public houses began to organise outings for their patrons

Outings organised by landlords for their regular customers began towards the end of the nineteenth century and were widespread by the interwar years. This outing, dated just prior to the First World War that started off from the *Star Hotel* at 138 Corve Street, shows the members of the Licensed Victuallers themselves ready for a trip. The landlord of the *Star Hotel*, Frederick William Curtis, stands in the foreground. (Courtesy of LHRG Archive)

The *New Inn* on New Street was a beerhouse. Though the police usually insisted on a landlord who could keep any customers who were a little worse for drink in order if necessary, this beerhouse had a landlady, Mrs Susan Crowther, seen here with her customers. Note the man on the left pouring a drink from a jug of beer that could be shared between friends.

(Courtesy of Shropshire Museum Service)

especially in the interwar years with the expansion of motor transport. The customers of the *Blue Boar* on Mill Street enjoyed an annual outing each year, with Symond's Yat being visited in 1932.[23]

One problem that publicans had was the belief in middle-class minds of the link between drink and violence. Every Christmas the *Horse and Jockey* on Holdgate Fee held a football match on the field behind with five or seven gallons of beer as a prize for the winning team. It was a popular event and 300-400 people would watch. In 1897, however, the game ended in a fight with not only just the players being involved but also with the watching crowd joining in. One court witness claimed 'the scene on that day was one of the most disgraceful that had ever taken place in Ludlow on the Lord's Day.' Though the police broke up the initial fracas, fighting carried on between two local families for the remainder of

the day.[24] This was not just an isolated case. Fighting outside public houses was a popular spectator sport but one that had unwritten rules to be followed.

Pub brawls and fights

Of the many cases that came to court, only a very few fights occurred inside a public house. It appeared that it was customary for the combatants involved to settle any dispute in the street outside so that no damage occurred within the confines of the local that might cause them to be banned. It helped that most landlords, and even their wives, were quite capable of evicting troublesome customers. In fact, the police tried to ensure that only those capable of controlling drunken patrons were granted licences. When Charles Powell wished to become landlord of the *Royal Oak* on Tower Street in 1896, the police objected on the grounds that he was not physically strong enough to control the type of customer who frequented that particular public house. As they pointed out to the magistrate:

> *'It required a very capable man as business done there was of a rough nature and required a physically capable man to look after it. Mr Powell was a man of small stature and would not make much impression on a man in drink.'*

In addition, his wife was described as 'a cripple' who would not be able to come to his aid. The licence was denied.[25]

Once outside, the men about to fight would first take off their jackets and sometimes their shirts. This was, no doubt, because most working-class men had few clothes and did not want them spoilt by either being torn or stained with blood. Word would soon spread, or sometimes the shouting and swearing of one or both of the participants would be heard. As a result crowds often gathered to watch the contest. This could range from 20-30 spectators or up to two hundred as occurred in Lower Galdeford in 1912 when a drunken Herbert Smith of Frog Lane offered to take on all-comers. A few months earlier a crowd of over fifty men, women and children watched and cheered whilst three men fought each other in Holdgate Fee. When it was women fighting, the crowds could gather even more quickly.[26]

When the police tried to break up such fights or arrest the fighters the crowd could themselves become involved. This could be by encouraging resistance or physically intervening to allow the combatants a chance to escape. When a police constable, who had already lost a tooth, attempted to arrest a man in Market Square, none of the 30-40 spectators whom he asked to help came to his aid.

At times the crowd did intervene but only to prolong the fun. On one occasion in Old Street the crowd grappled the policeman to the ground and he had to be rescued by a fellow officer using his truncheon. In the meantime the original troublemaker made his getaway. When the policemen then tried to arrest one member of the crowd, who had taken off his belt and was swinging it around as a weapon, the remainder once again stood back to watch and cheer him on.

An even larger confrontation took place outside the *Green Dragon* on Old Street. A crowd of over 150 gathered to stop a policeman arresting a drunken man. In the melee the constable lost both his whistle and his handcuffs and it was only when four further policemen arrived on the scene that the arrested man was taken, with great difficulty, through the gathering crowd to the police station. Once inside the incident did not end. Over two hundred people, many of them women, remained outside 'hooting the police'.[27]

In a later court appearance, the local police superintendent explained to the magistrate the difficulty that such crowd behaviour caused them. Giving evidence regarding the arrest of another drunk in Old Street who had to be manhandled to the police station he stated, 'he did not think the prisoner would have been so bad had he not been encouraged by the crowd.'[28]

Such spectacles were witnessed in the interwar years. At the top of Galdeford, two men, stripped of their jackets, fought in the street watched by a cheering crowd of 40-50, whilst in Holdgate Fee a crowd of at least 100 men, women and children collected to view a fight after an argument in the *Horse and Jockey* public house.[29]

Such unruly behaviour, seen so often on Ludlow's streets, was anathema to the town's 'respectable' citizens. To try and bring it to an end, a number of strategies were followed up to 1914. One was the formulation of a blacklist. Placed on this were those who were habitually coming before the magistrate's bench on charges of drunkenness and breaches of the peace. In 1906 it was decided that anyone convicted of drunkenness four times in twelve months would be placed on such a blacklist for three years. This would mean that they could not be served a drink in any public house. Three persons

Even in 1950 public houses tended to cater for a certain type of customer and the *Smithfield* on Lower Galdeford was a typical working-class public house. Here four such customers pose for a photograph at its entrance including Edward (Ted) Bradley on the left and James Francis on the right.

(Courtesy of Caroline Thomas and John Palmer)

were immediately placed on it including a William Marsh of Frog Lane. A photograph and details of each individual was circulated to all landlords both in Ludlow and the surrounding villages. Women were not excluded and a Margaret Bursnell of Lower Galdeford was placed on the list in 1912. Any publican found serving any of those blacklisted would suffer a fine of £2 plus court costs. A blacklist was still in operation in the interwar years.[30]

Magistrates' Court reports show that the number of alcohol-induced fights in the town's streets fell during the interwar years, though with the rise of the dance halls, as will be seen in Chapter 5, a fresh venue for such violence was seen. Fighting as a spectator sport saw a resurgence in the Second World War when hundreds, and at times thousands, of servicemen flooded into Ludlow. Drunkenness and rowdyism at Town Hall dances grew so bad that local residents complained to the council. They claimed that after each dance some 200-300 men, women and even girls as young as fifteen, were ejected out onto the streets, many of them in a drunken state and that this often resulted in a number of fights. For some of the town's youth this fighting brought vicarious pleasure. 'Any bit of dancing and… it was mayhem. A couple of pints and that was it. They would fight anybody. We used to sit in Woolworth's doorway to see the action.'[31] This did not alter when peace came. When a local man was charged with being drunk and threatening fellow dancers with a beer bottle, the police superintendent claimed his force was being stretched virtually to breaking point:

> *'We have had a considerable amount of trouble at the Town Hall at the Saturday night dances and there are certain elements that come here after the public houses turn out and we have had to police at the Town Hall instead of patrolling the streets. I should like your worship's assistance to prevent this reprehensible conduct going on … Often too, trouble was caused by people who could not get into the dances.'*[32]

Holdgate Fee was the scene of a number of fights between people the worse for drink especially outside the *Horse and Jockey* and *Hen and Chickens* public houses. Crowds, sometimes totalling three figures, would pour out of the houses to watch and even to hinder the police who would be trying to pull the combatants apart and arrest them. Fights between women drew particularly large crowds.
(Courtesy of Shropshire Museum Service)

Fighting in Ludlow's streets, away from the dance halls, also carried on after the war, at times fuelled by drink. A feud between the Marsh and Bradley families erupted in Old Street when six men were involved in a violent confrontation, leaving one of them with two broken legs. Citizens that came out of their houses to watch the fight were reticent when asked to give evidence in the witness box. To laughter in the public section of the court, each witness claimed that they had failed to see who struck whom and when, as their attention at that moment had been distracted or that they had been tending the injured. For the same reason no one saw anyone wield an iron bar or similar weapon. But as for how common such fights around the town were, the plea from the police superintendent to the bench is telling.

> *'I ask your worships to deal with the defendants with severity. There is too much of this sort of thing going on in the town at the present time.'*[33]

Gambling

In the nineteenth and early twentieth century, magistrates also saw the public house as a place where working-class men could become addicted to gambling and squander the limited income that was needed to house, feed and clothe their family. Stopping gambling, they believed, would reduce the numbers applying for poor relief that was funded by middle-class ratepayers. As a

The north side of Upper Galdeford was the site of a number of public houses two of which survived into the second half of the twentieth century: The *Three Horse Shoes* and the *Portcullis*. As part of constant attempts to stamp down on gambling in public houses, in 1902 the police hid all day behind the *Portcullis Inn* to observe customers playing skittles for pints of ale. As a result fifteen men, including the landlord Thomas Rogers, were charged and fined. (Courtesy of Shropshire Museum Service)

result, even gambling for small stakes both inside and outside public houses had to be discouraged.

Four youngsters from Lower Galdeford and Lower Mill Street discovered gambling for pennies on Castle Walks found themselves in court. Each was given a choice of a 5/- fine or five days in prison. The evidence was one young man trying to hide seven pennies in his mouth and a halfpenny found under the seat they were using. Three youths were fined for playing pitch-and-toss under the light of a lamp post in Lower Galdeford. The magistrate warned them that such an activity 'was one that led unquestionably to dishonesty and trouble.'[34] The clampdown on such games carried on into the interwar years. Seven young men caught playing pitch-and-toss in Portcullis Lane were fined 5/- each and on the same day three others were fined for playing cards for money, also in Portcullis Lane.[35]

Ending gambling in public houses, however small the stakes, was something that the magistrates thought important and constantly instructed the police to clamp down on. The landlord of the *Nelson Inn* at Rocks Green, along with four customers, was prosecuted for allowing the playing of bagatelle where the losers bought a pint of beer for the victors.[36] It was the same as regards the playing of cards and dominoes that were both very popular in local public houses. Middle-class magistrates believed even these pastimes encouraged ill-afforded betting and asked the police to take a firmer view of the practice. They also demanded publicans 'not to allow cards or domino playing to take place' anywhere on their premises.[37]

The police often went to great lengths to catch customers gambling. The *Portcullis Inn* had an outside skittle alley and in the summer of 1902, two policemen hid themselves in the early hours of the morning where they had a clear view of the skittle alley. They somehow managed to remain hidden all day until after closing time making copious notes of all games played. As a result, Thomas Rogers, the publican, and fourteen

The 1904 Licensing Act allowed magistrates, on police advice, to recommend the closure of certain public houses in the knowledge that the Government would compensate a publican for their loss of livelihood. In the case of the *Bell Inn* at the bottom of Lower Broad Street, the reason given by the police for its closure was that it had at least five possible escape routes if it were ever raided due to fighting or illegal drinking.

(Courtesy of Shropshire Museum Service)

of his customers found themselves in court being given the choice of a fine or up to fourteen days in prison with hard labour for playing skittles for a pint or a quart to the winner.[38]

Illegal gambling was not, of course, linked solely to the public house, though most taking part appear to belong to the working-classes. Bets could be laid and taken legally on a racecourse, but off-course betting was outlawed in 1853 and remained illegal until 1960. A number of local shopkeepers, however, were willing to take bets. In 1905, John Daulby, a saddler with a shop in the Bull Ring, was charged with accepting bets from a bootboy at the *Feathers Hotel*. He had been seen entering the shop on numerous of occasions with bets for a number of people. These included his fellow workers such as the underboots, a chambermaid and a coffee room waitress, as well as for the brewer at the *Globe* public house on Market Street. The extent of the problem can be seen when the police asked the magistrates for an example to be made in order to deter many other illegal bookmakers that they believed were widespread in Ludlow.[39]

Street betting also occurred. In 1931 Joseph Collier of Friars Terrace, Old Street, was observed by police next to the Buttercross and in the High Street, accepting slips of paper and envelopes from a number of men and women. Cash was also seen to change hands. After his arrest several betting slips were found on him and £10 in cash. Joseph pleaded guilty and was fined £5. [40]

Attempts to close down public houses

A reduction in the actual number of public houses was another solution that was constantly pursued in order to reduce what was viewed as the detrimental drinking habits of the lower orders. Due to the intense competition amongst the 72 public houses that graced the town in 1850, some fell by the wayside due to landlords being unable to make a living. Magistrates also managed to close a few others when the police convicted landlords for breaking the law or keeping unruly houses. They were pleased to report in 1878 that in the previous twelve years, 14 public houses in Ludlow had closed. However, by 1890 there was still one for every 93 people in the borough.

The breakthrough came with the Licensing Act of 1904 by which the Government hoped to encourage a reduction in the number of public houses with the setting up of a fund to compensate landlords who would lose their livelihoods. This gave the police and the magistrates the opportunity that they had been waiting for and they accepted it with alacrity. In 1907 five public houses were recommended for closure: the *Bell Inn* on Upper Galdeford, the *Black Boy* on Tower Street, the *Castle Tavern* on Old Street, *The Grapes* on Market Street and the *Imperial Vaults* on the corner of Old Street and the Bull Ring. The reasons given by the police were the proximity of other public houses, poor trade, poor accommodation and the lack of sanitary facilities.

It is interesting to note, however, that as regards the *Black Boy,* a further reason given was that there were too many alleys nearby where persons could evade arrest. It was the same as regards the closure of the *Bell Inn* on Lower Broad Street. The police objected to the renewal of its licence because it had five possible entrances and escape routes that could be used to avoid arrest for out-of-hours drinking or violent disturbance.[41] Other closures soon followed. By 1914, among others, the *Cross Keys* on St Mary's Lane and the *Plough Inn* on Raven Lane had

As an alternative to visiting the public house, the Rector of St Laurence Church together with other prominent local men, opened in 1903 an Evening Club above the Buttercross. Here, for a very small fee, men could socialise, read and play games such as dominoes, darts and bagatelle away from the temptation of alcoholic drink. (Courtesy of Shropshire Museum Service)

closed their doors and the total number of public houses in Ludlow, compared to 1850, had been halved. This attack on the number of public houses in the town did not halt and a number of others were forced to shut down in the interwar years. By the time that the *Trotting Horse* on Corve Street was made to close its doors in 1937, the number had been reduced to 29. By 1941 this was 28, compared to 72 in 1850.[42]

Another tactic to reduce what a number saw as the detrimental influence of drink on working-class life was to try to woo the young men of the town away from public houses by offering them relaxation and the chance to play pub games in comfortable surroundings where alcohol was not served. An Evening Club was set up in the Buttercross in 1903. The Rector of St Laurence stated openly that the purpose of this club was to give working men an alternative to the public house. George Woolley, a printer and bookseller, who was appointed secretary and treasurer, explained that 'one of the best means of fighting excessive drinking, and training men to find social companionship otherwise than in the public house' was by offering them an enjoyable alternative.[43]

This was not the first time that the provision of an Evening Club had been attempted. But the first, organised by local churchmen in 1863 was, as will be seen in Chapter 3, part of the overall movement of encouraging self-improvement amongst the working-classes. The club offered its members, at a cost of 2d per week or 1d per night, somewhere warm to go in the winter evenings between 7pm and 10pm. Here, 'for this trifling amount,' chess and draughts could be played and newspapers, periodicals and a 'well appointed and well selected library' was available to them. In addition, members were entertained to musical recitals on the piano and violin and could also listen to readings from Shakespeare. The club lasted until the 1890s when it closed due to a waning of interest. The lure of the public house had not been tamed.[44]

The club's resurrection in 1903, with its new aim of offering a more realistic and tempting alternative to the public house, ensured that its offerings were more in tune with the needs of its desired members. As before, the club was open nightly for thirty weeks of the year during the winter months from 7pm to 10pm. Once again a season ticket could be purchased for 3/6d, a weekly ticket for 2d or a nightly one for 1d. As before, somewhere warm and comfortable was offered with hot drinks and reading materials. This time, however, games, normally found in public houses, were offered including ringboard, bagatelle, dominoes, indoor quoits and billiards.

Tournaments were even organised complete with prizes. Card games such as whist and cribbage were allowed though any gambling would result in instant expulsion. The Evening Club prospered, attracting 35–40 men each session and was still in existence during the interwar years, only finally closing its doors in 1946 as the rival temptations of the wireless, dance halls and the cinema wooed the last of its membership away.[45]

The temperance movement

Another string to the middle-class bow was their support for the temperance movement which advocated total abstinence from alcohol. This movement helped exert pressure on both councillors and magistrates when making their decisions.

The temperance movement in Ludlow was always quite powerful and a few establishments opened to cater for men and women who wanted somewhere to stay where alcohol was not served. After closure, the *Royal Oak* public house at 13 Tower Street was reopened in 1900 as the *Royal Oak Café and Temperance Hotel.* As this advertisement shows, it offered a different form of accommodation to, among others, commercial travellers and touring cyclists.

(Courtesy of Shropshire Museum Service)

Until 1914, Ludlow saw a number of local branches of national temperance organisations hold meetings in the town such as the Working Men's Temperance Society, the Church of England Temperance Society (which even had its own boys section) and the British Women's Temperance Association. This latter group organised the serving of tea in the Assembly Rooms at the time of the May Fair in an attempt to wean customers away from the public houses.

A procession organised by members of the Total Abstinence Society, led by a band, toured the streets before making its way onto Whitcliffe for a rally and tea in a large tent. Other groups took more militant action. The Gospel Temperance Army also embarked on marches through the streets of Ludlow, lustily singing temperance songs and handing out blue ribbons to those they persuaded to give up drink. But also, as their name suggests, they took the battle directly to the drinkers. In Holdgate Fee, 150 of their members laid siege to the *Hen and Chickens* public house. To the accompaniment of the beating of a drum they sang, preached and harangued customers trying to enter. The landlord took them to court but the magistrates, perhaps showing their sympathies, dismissed the case, thus encouraging yet further direct action.[46]

The introduction of prohibition in the USA in 1920, when the production, sale and consumption of alcohol was made illegal, reinvigorated the temperance movement in the United Kingdom. A branch of the Total Abstinence League was formed in Ludlow. In addition, a Ludlow Band of Hope was planned. Started in 1847 by the Reverend Jabez Tunnicliff, a Baptist Minister in Leeds, this three million-strong organisation offered children activities that would encourage them to avoid intoxicants.

Battle lines began to form as anti-prohibition meetings were held in the town square. Even the Mayor in 1920 said that people should have the freedom to drink alcohol if they wished though, admittedly, Edward Sheldon was a publican. In 1922 the League of Freedom and Reform held a public meeting in Castle Square. Speeches requested that churches should refrain from entering the debate. It was argued that prohibition, or even a large reduction in the number of public houses or the hours that they served, was an attack on the leisure habits of the working-classes. Meanwhile, the hypocrisy of some was alluded to when it was pointed out that the middle-classes could still stock their cellars.

The League's solution to worries about the detrimental effects of the present public house system was to encourage landlords and brewers to persuade more women to enter them by making the premises more welcoming. In addition, licensed premises should be encouraged to provide food in addition to drink. The result, it was believed, would be to improve the image of the public house and moderate both excessive drinking and boisterous behaviour.[47]

However, local attempts to improve facilities for customers still came up against both temperance and public order pressures. When the *Three Horseshoes* on Upper Galdeford sought permission for building alterations, they had to give

In 1926 the *Golden Lion Hotel* at 12, Old Street (now Trevor Lloyd, Bookbinder and Restorer) gave up its licence and became the *Lion Temperance Hotel* with William Downs as its proprietor.

This effort to offer an alternative to the town's other hotels was short lived as it closed in the mid 1930s.

(Courtesy of Tony Hobbs)

assurances to the magistrates' bench that the work 'did not give increased facilities for drinking or conceal any part of the premises.' Even when the *Ludlow Arms* on Whitcliffe, the home of the Whitcliffe Bowls Club whose membership was decidedly middle-class, required permission to remove the kitchen range and replace it with a 'nice fire grate and redecorate,' the landlord had to emphasise that there was no intention of 'increasing drinking facilities.' An application by the landlord of the *Smithfield Inn* on Lower Galdeford to extend the smoke room by incorporating the old brew house also found himself having to defend his proposed action. He explained that the door to the smoke room would now be moved to opposite the bar so that he could keep a better eye on the behaviour of his customers. Even so the final decision went up as far as the Chief Constable.[48]

Other evidence of the continuing influence of the temperance movement in Ludlow can be seen in the conversion of the *Golden Lion Hotel* on Old Street into the *Lion Temperance Hotel* in 1926. It also became quite common for those charged

Originally public houses brewed and sold their own beer though this began to change once the national brewery companies expanded at the end of the nineteenth century and tied houses started to become the norm. In Ludlow a number of inns still carried on brewing as this advertisement for the *Three Horse Shoes* on Upper Galdeford proudly boasts.
(Courtesy of LHRG Archive)

By the outbreak of the Second World War the number of public houses still brewing their own beer had dwindled considerably and, in the late 1940s, the *Wheatsheaf Inn* at the top of Lower Broad Street was the last to do so.

with drunkenness, or fighting due to intoxication, to inform the presiding magistrate that they had taken 'the pledge,' no doubt in the hope that a more lenient punishment might be given. One decision by the magistrates had an unforeseen effect rather than the one they had desired. The usual request for an alcohol licence for the annual Territorials' Dance at the Town Hall was refused. The result was that 'unfortunately there was not a very large attendance.' No doubt with their ears burning, the magistrates agreed to all further applications.[49]

Reduced hours of opening

Surprisingly, it was the invasion of Belgium by the German Army in August 1914 that had the most dramatic influence on the drinking habits of Ludlow, as it did on the rest of Britain. This was as regards public house hours of opening. Hours when alcohol could be served on Sundays had already been limited

CHAPTER 3

Further Attempts to 'Civilise' the Crowd

There appears to have been a concerted effort to 'civilise' the working-classes of Ludlow and to mould their leisure pursuits down a more 'respectable' path. As well as the curtailment of a number of traditional pursuits and an attempt to reduce what was seen as the detrimental influence of the public house, three further major routes to attain this goal can be discerned: various efforts by church and chapel, the inculcation of team spirit through organised sport, and the encouragement of working-class organisations that required a committee structure.

Attempts by the various religious bodies to mould the habits of a future generation started with the birth of a number of children's organisations. The Sunday School Movement began in the eighteenth century in order to teach reading, writing and arithmetic, as well as bible study, to children who worked all week. In the beginning the schools were for all children, be they church or chapel. The first such school in Ludlow opened in 1844 over the old market hall in Castle

Sunday School children would sometimes be taken out for treats such as magic lantern slide shows. This group, alongside their teachers, have been assembled at the Town Hall in 1922, wearing their best clothes, for a similar event. (Courtesy of LHRG Archive)

Square. It was for boys at first but a section for girls opened the following year. Between them they soon had a joint membership of 500.

However, this example of Christian brotherhood and unity soon came to an end. The competition for the souls of the town brought about a schism, with churches and chapels opening their own competing Sunday schools. As well as aiding in basic education these schools also gave the children the chance to take part in a number of social activities. The year 1862 shows both the growing schism in the Sunday School Movement and evidence of outings that the children now enjoyed. The children from the Wesleyan Chapel on Lower Broad Street walked in procession to the railway station to board the 10am train to Church Stretton where they enjoyed the hills, played games and sat down to tea and cakes. Those attending the Independent Church Sunday school on Old Street enjoyed plum cake before walking to a field at Ludford for an afternoon of fun and games until the 'sun went down.' Meanwhile the members of the Primitive Methodist Chapel Sunday school, also on Old Street, after they had enjoyed tea and cake, went off to Whitcliffe to play games.[1] Alongside these Sunday schools, the Congregational Church and the Trinity Free Church also competed for children's attendance, the latter utilising the Templars' Hall in Brand Lane. The Church of England, which had opened the National School

For many children, especially those from the poorer areas of town, Sunday School outings were often the only time they ever saw sights outside of Ludlow. This outing for children, organised by the Gospel Hall off Old Street, would have also seen them playing games and having a picnic or a party meal at a local chapel before being brought home. (Courtesy of LHRG Archive)

on Lower Galdeford and later a second one at East Hamlet, used these buildings for their own Sunday schools, expecting all pupils to attend.

After school attendance was made compulsory in 1870, the various Sunday schools moved away from teaching basic education to more enjoyable learning experiences, though ones with a distinct religious message. As the years passed, Sunday school outings became more of a public celebration and a chance to sell their individual messages to the town at large. Colourful processions became the norm, often headed by a band, and complete with banners. Having the largest Sunday School Movement, the Church of England led the way. On the days of its annual treat, the walk from the two Ludlow National Schools met up for a combined march through the centre of the town. The turnout of up to one thousand children was enhanced by the inclusion of children from church schools in local villages. The older children would attend a service at St Laurence whilst the infants sat down to a tea in the Town Hall. After the service the elder boys and girls also went to the Town Hall for their tea, the boys sitting downstairs and the girls upstairs. Tables were covered with 'snowy white tablecloths decorated with flowers and laid with jugs filled with tea and plates of bread and butter that later were followed by cakes and buns.' All the children then walked to the Castle Green to take part in sports and to be entertained by a Punch and Judy Show and a conjuror.[2] The overall effect of such a day on the children, who would often return home to a one-up-one down cottage, often damp and lit by a single gaslight or even candles, can be imagined. The message was simple: Christian respectability offered the possible reward of a better life.

By the turn of the twentieth century, in terms of numbers, the Sunday School Movement had reached its zenith.[3] A rethink was required as to how to keep attracting the young. The result was that as well as looking at what was on offer on Sundays, the churches spread their net even wider and now began offering both children and young adults midweek recreational facilities. The Congregational Church held weekly winter evenings for children where lantern slide shows could be enjoyed and singsongs held. Children were also encouraged to bring a friend with them. The church also set up a Monday Evening Club for girls over the age of fourteen where music and needlework were two of the activities on offer.[4] Efforts were made to offer young adults clubs to join. A Free Church Recreation Club was begun in 1905 and later renamed St Julian's Recreational Club. The club rented a field next to Overmead, off Livesey Road, the home of Gaius Smith, the one-time mayor and the high-class grocer whose main shop was on Broad Street. The membership tended to

Thanks to the railways, Sunday School outings sometimes travelled far from the town. This Methodist Sunday School trip in 1898 saw this large group of children and their helpers taken to the perhaps inappropriately named Devil's Bridge Falls in mid-Wales.
(Courtesy of Steven Edwards)

The Boys' Brigade was a Church of England youth organisation that had a Ludlow branch with its headquarters at St Stephen's Hall off Upper Galdeford. Here they are forming a guard of honour for Princess Mary as she leaves St Laurence Church in 1909.

be made up of the lower middle-class: young shop assistants and the sons and daughters of small tradesmen whose social aspirations can be seen in the sports and games chosen: cricket, bowls, tennis and croquet, the latter two played on the lawns that fronted Overmead.[5]

Adults had not been forgotten. In 1863, at the instigation of the Rector of St Laurence and other local clergy, an Evening Club was opened in the room above the Buttercross. Its aim was for the 'improvement of the working-classes' though only men could join. It was open every evening during the winter months for a small charge of 1d per night or 2d for the week. How the club was to encourage self-improvement can be seen when it was said that 'for this trifling amount, newspapers, periodicals, chess, draughts etc. are supplied and members also have a use of a well arranged and well selected library.' By 'well selected' it was

Stretching into the interwar years, local nonconformists organised an annual open-air meeting on Whitcliffe each year with chapelgoers from the surrounding area joining local congregations to listen to invited preachers. It was also a looked forward to social event with some families camping out overnight.
(Courtesy of Shropshire Museum Service)

meant that all books conveyed a high moral Christian stance.[6] Further evidence of how the middle-class organisers hoped to encourage self-improvement can be seen in the programme of the entertainment provided for the members. This was held at the market hall every two or three weeks during the autumn and winter months and they participated in music recitals on the piano and violin, readings, including extracts from Shakespeare, and songs. The club lasted until the 1890s when falling attendance led to its closure.[7]

Other church organisations were set up to cater for the intellectual self-improvement of its members based on Christian principles. The Primitive Methodist Church on Old Street offered men a PSA (Pleasant Sunday Afternoon) Club in 1905, where members would listen to lectures and sing hymns. Unfortunately, due to lack of support, the gatherings folded three years later. More successful was the Ludlow Branch of the Men's Own Brotherhood, one of many that were being formed throughout Britain. At its inaugural meeting in 1910 all churches were invited and the Rector of St Laurence asked to be its president. However, once again religious competition in the form of church versus chapel held sway and he turned down the invitation, citing too many commitments. As a result, the Church of England did not become involved. Instead it set up a rival organisation called the Church of England Men's Society that met on a Sunday afternoon. After a religious service the forty members would be treated to a religious lecture. Meanwhile the Brotherhood attracted 150 men to its first meeting in the Assembly Rooms, a number that soon rose to two hundred in the following months. Meetings then moved to the British School in Old Street. Here members would listen

The ethos of the Boys' Brigade was based on semi-military discipline and physical fitness. As well as regular local meetings throughout the year they set off for a week's annual camp under canvas. As can be seen in this photograph from the 1912 camp, rifle practice was one skill they practised. Note also that at least one officer is wearing his clerical collar.

Photographed in 1910 this is the first Ludlow Scout troop to be formed. Because of the cost of the uniform these early members tended to be the children of the middle-classes as can be discerned from their well-nourished appearance. (Courtesy Ludlow Museum Service)

to talks, often on topical issues of the day, interspersed with scripture readings and the singing of hymns.[8]

Edward Burrows, a man of private means, waxed lyrical about the perceived success of the Ludlow Brotherhood, claiming that it was 'doing splendid work in the town. It has reached men that churches have failed to touch. The absence of formality and stiffness has contributed in great measure to its success.' However, its mainly lower middle-class membership and its failure to attract working-class support brought criticism. A letter to the *Ludlow Advertiser* argued that for all the meetings, lectures and discussions of white slavery, temperance and other similar topics little was learned of real value as regards understanding the local community. Middle-class knowledge of the true everyday lives of the working-classes was still completely lacking. It was claimed that organisers and members would learn far more of real importance if they actually visited a working-class public house for a drink of beer or water where 'they would be surprised to learn how little they knew' of working-class life.[9]

Also to be seen were attempts by the churches to try to distract working-class men from frequenting the public house by offering then leisure opportunities away from the temptation of drink. In 1875 the Ludlow Men's Church Society was set up with the aim of reducing drunkenness in the town by inviting men to the market hall to a supper followed by singing and general entertainment.[10] It was not successful. Of greater success, as was seen in Chapter 2, was the rebirth in 1903 of the Evening Club above the Buttercross where members were now offered all the games that they could find in the public house but without the alcohol.

Women were not totally forgotten, but this was the time when the belief of 'separate spheres' held sway: that the world of work was for men whilst the place for women was in the home. The churches therefore offered clubs based around housewifery skills, with the Primitive Methodist Chapel holding a weekly Ladies' Sewing Class, though they now and again held social evenings of song and humour. In addition, the Church of England opened a branch of the Mothers' Union that met above the Buttercross. Originally founded in 1876 to train women of all classes in motherhood skills, it rapidly became a national movement in the 1890s, though one more interested in attempts to correct social ills. The Ludlow branch mainly became a middle-class group that met together to listen to invited guests speaking on various moral issues.[11]

Church outings

Women could, of course, take part in the family outings that the churches began to offer. These were usually under the auspices of the various Sunday schools with parents, especially mothers, encouraged to accompany their children in order to help in the day's fun. Such trips may have started off in a simple fashion such as with the Primitive Methodists in 1867 organising an excursion for two hundred children and adults to Titterstone Clee Hill by horse-drawn carriage, with games followed by tea before returning to Ludlow for yet more games. Two years before, however, a glimpse of the future was seen when the Old Street Methodist school outing went by train to Knighton for sports and a tea at the local Methodist chapel.[12] Soon train trips were the norm with the Wesleyan and Congregational Sunday school's annual trip in 1880 to Church Stretton for games, followed by tea at the Carding Mill Glen.

Outings soon grew more adventurous with the annual Wesleyan outing taking pride of place. In 1900, two hundred children, parents and friends travelled by a specially chartered train to Llandrindod Wells. They enjoyed boating on the lake followed by tea and then more boating before setting off back to Ludlow. 1902 saw 500 passengers travel to Aberystwyth, whilst in 1904 'several hundreds' enjoyed Barmouth. In 1905, 450

Sir Robert Baden-Powell, the founder of the Boy Scout movement visited Ludlow Castle in 1910 to inspect the various South Shropshire Troops watched by one thousand spectators that included many proud parents. (Courtesy of Ludlow Museum Service)

In the years just after the First World War a Girl Guide troop was also formed in Ludlow. As with the Boy Scouts, due to the cost of the uniforms, the early members tended to be from middle or lower middle-class families. (Courtesy of Shropshire Museum Service)

men, women and children set off to Bristol and Weston-Super-Mare. These large numbers occurred because the outings were opened up to the entire populace of the town so that the profits could be used to subsidise the Sunday school children and their families, many of whom were from the poorer sections of the working-classes. The day out was a great success.

> *'Visitors found the resort bathed in sunshine …. The piers, parks and promenades, to say nothing of the varied amusements on the sands, proved great attractions. Bathing and boating were also indulged in to the heart's content, while many, as well as enjoying several pleasant hours in Weston, managed to get across the Bristol channel to a place on the South Wales coast, thanks to the excellent steamboat service.'* [13]

For children and parents, who otherwise may not have been able to leave the confines of their home town, the message was unchanged: Christian worship brought its rewards.

Boys' Brigade and Boy Scout movement

Branches of national organisations supported by the church also flourished. A branch of the Boys' Brigade was formed in the town with its headquarters in St Stephen's Hall. Originally formed in Glasgow in 1883, its aim was to develop Christian Manliness in young men through semi-military discipline, sport and summer camps, combined with religious services and instruction. During the Edwardian years the local group had an airgun range, held boxing competitions and went on annual camps where they joined other brigades. In 1911 this was at Rhyl. The boys were continually weighed and measured to show how exercise improved their physique.[14]

A Ludlow troop of the Boy Scout Movement was formed in 1909 just one year after the national movement was set up by Sir Robert Baden-Powell. Again, physical fitness with military overtones was to the fore. The boys converted a small barn next to the Drill Hall on Portcullis Lane into a gymnasium, whilst they also had use of the rifle range next door. Swimming competitions in the River Teme were also organised. As with the Boys' Brigade, annual camps were attended. At Towyn, in 1910, they joined other local troops and camped by the seashore. On their final day a battle was arranged when half the boys were ordered to attack the camp whilst the other half defended. On their return to Ludlow the mayor, who welcomed them home, said that the Germans would never invade if they saw the scouts in action.[15]

In 1910, Ludlow hosted a visit from Sir Robert Baden-Powell himself in the castle grounds. 179 boys from South Shropshire Scout troops attended watched by one thousand spectators. In a show of their military training, the scouts suddenly rushed out from their hiding places to great applause. Like the Boys' Brigade, however, the Scouts tended to be the sons of the professional and employer classes, partly due to the cost of joining. They realised this themselves with the troop in

1913 planning to raise monies to help poorer families pay for their child's uniform.[16]

When war broke out in August 1914 the two organisations were ready to play their part. The Ludlow Scout Troop was sent to set up camp at Bromfield and were given the responsibility of guarding the railway line between Ludlow and Church Stretton from possible sabotage by enemy agents. The local Boys' Brigade were given the task of helping to guard seventy miles of the Birmingham water supply line and were camped at Kidderminster. Then in December 1914 they were ordered to the Elan Valley in Wales to take over the protection of the reservoirs there. When the boys reached the

As part of the Muscular Christianity movement that emanated from the public schools, both the established church and nonconformists set up football teams for the younger male members of their congregations. This is the Wesleyan FC who played on a ground at the Linney in the 1903/04 season.
(Courtesy of Shropshire Museum Service)

Ludlow Athletic FC was one of the cup winners during the 1897/98 season. This was just one of many clubs that were formed locally in the late 19th century as both the lower middle and working-classes of the town took to the sport though not always with the attitude that playing the game for its own sake was more important than the winning.

age of eighteen they then volunteered for the army.[17] Both organisations carried on locally in peacetime though the Scout troop had to be reformed in 1921 whilst the early 1920s saw the Girl Guides and the Brownies formed in the town.

Muscular Christianity

The church also encouraged the formation of football teams with St Laurence FC and St John's Rovers FC playing games in the 1880s. This was based on the perceived virtues of 'Muscular Christianity,' a philosophy that originated in the mid nineteenth century as a method of building character amongst boys in English public schools. It was a belief that participation in sport could contribute to the development, not only of physical fitness but also of Christian morals, through good sportsmanship and putting the team before oneself. It was based on the premise that 'A manly boy was strong of body and pure of heart.' Young men who had returned from public school education, or who had attended the local grammar school that in many ways attempted to copy public school ways and traditions, brought such ideas to Ludlow.[18]

At the Ludlow Grammar School Speech Day in 1903, the Headmaster, Reverend Hastings, eulogised 'the enormous advantages, physical and moral, of entering heartily into school sport.' The headmaster also practised what he preached as he was a keen member of the town's cricket team.[19] Herbert Allcroft of Stokesay Court echoed such a sentiment when he addressed the Ludlow Town Football Club's annual dinner in

Ludlow Thursday FC were also cup winners in the 1897/98 season. They were made up of shop workers who tended to play on Thursday afternoons when local businesses had their half-day closing. Early attempts to amalgamate local teams to form a stronger Ludlow FC failed due to class prejudice with manual workers refusing to play with such men whom they saw as not being true members of the working-class.

(Courtesy of Shropshire Museum Service)

1910 dressed in his hunting pink, the club colours. He told them that playing the game in the true spirit 'led to manliness,' 'obedience' and the ability 'to keep your temper.' In a similar vein HT Weyman intoned, before the Church Lads Brigade kicked off at their new Bromfield ground in 1923:

> *'May they play in the true English spirit, in the spirit of sportsmanship and not for the self, for the team to which they belong. The team must always come before any personal ends of their own.'* [20]

From the late nineteenth century there was a desire by the town's social elite to try to instil such values in the working-classes, believing that it would help put them on the road to self-improvement. It was hoped that association football could be utilised in this way and certainly the young people of the town took the game to their hearts and teams proliferated. There were the Ludlow Castle Swifts, Ludlow Stars, Ludlow Thistle, Ludlow Amateurs, Ludlow Athletics, Ludlow St George's and Ludlow Thursday among many others. Sadly, the aim to promote sportsmanship and fair play through such a team game was not totally successful.

In 1898 when St George's were playing Knighton, the entire team, angered after the referee awarded a Knighton goal after what they saw as an obvious and deliberate hand ball, refused to carry on playing and walked off the pitch. Tension between teams often spilt over to affect the watching crowd. When Ludlow Stars played Ludlow Castle Swifts, ill feeling between the clubs resulted in one spectator running onto the pitch to kick the right wing of the Stars team. Opposing supporters were only just stopped from throwing the man into the River Teme. When Ludlow Town played Hereford in a replayed cup match the referee was attacked and struck as well as being 'hit with a clod or some such missile.'[21]

The concept of putting the team before self was another lesson lost on a number of players. Ludlow Town FC often found themselves in difficulties in their earlier years, both financially and as regards player numbers. Players constantly switched clubs preferring a team that was more generous with expenses or which had a greater chance of winning cups.[22]

Class divisions were also far from healed by this rise in the popularity of team sport. When, in 1898, there was a call for three local working-class clubs, St George's FC, Ludlow Athletic and Ludlow Thursday, to amalgamate so that the town could have a stronger team to represent them, the effort fell at the first hurdle. St George FC refused to discuss the proposal, claiming that they were the only true working-class team of the three, as all their players were manual labourers, whereas those of the other two teams were shop assistants or clerks.

As for the middle-class youth of Ludlow, who had initially supported working-class participation in the game, they, as will be seen in the next chapter, now switched to other sports that the working-class would find more difficult to join in, such as hockey and tennis.

Though many of the middle-class youth moved away from association football, their fathers did not. Organising, managing and sponsoring a successful football team brought popularity that for some was especially valuable at election time. When a team won a cup and were met at the station by a cheering crowd, such men could bask in their reflected glory.

At first local worthies chaired and sat on the committees of local clubs, helped with travel costs, the payment of rent for pitches and for their football kit. By the interwar years, financial support was more substantial with ground improvements to the fore. Thanks to the support of 'local gentry and tradesmen of the district,' Ludlow Town FC, who then played on land just off Julian Road, had 'one of the best grounds in the district.' It was 'equipped with covered stand for the comfort of ladies and aged supporters, (and) a pay office for the comfort of gatemen at the entrance.' It also boasted 'accommodation for home and visiting teams with bath comforts, heating and lighting, also separate room for the referee.'[23]

Foot races and field competitions in the form of sprinting and jumping had been participated in by all classes and by all ages and were an integral part of local fetes and galas. However, for the working-classes this was often not sport for sports sake. Such competition usually went hand

Though it was possible to learn to box from the late nineteenth century the sport really took off in Ludlow in 1933. Pictured here are two brothers with the many cups that they had won, often donated by local dignitaries: Jackie Collier, a middleweight, and Archie Collier, a welterweight.

The Boxing Club had its early headquarters at the *New Inn* on Upper Galdeford but the rapid expansion of its membership caused it to move its practice sessions to the *Eagle* on Corve Street and then to the *Queens Hotel* at the top of Lower Galdeford in 1936. (Courtesy of Shropshire Museum Service)

in hand with cash prizes, wagers and side betting. In 1863 a 100 yard sprint between two local men for a £5 bet, starting at the Corve Gate at 7pm in the evening, attracted a crowd numbering 1,500. Apparently, widespread betting amongst the spectators was the norm. This was their second race the first being won by Caleb Spear, a house painter. It was noted at the time 'there was not so much (side) betting as at the last race about five weeks ago' and Spear 'is now termed the champion of Ludlow.' Such races, over various distances, for prize money were still prevalent in the 1880s though they now tended to take place along the Bromfield Road.[24]

At times there were races with a difference, but always for valuable awards. A wheelbarrow race for a number of prizes was held in 1910. The rules were that the barrows had to have one wheel, no straps or ropes and 1 cwt of coal had to be carried and returned. The race would start at the Star Vaults and go down Corve Street to the Felton turn off on the Bromfield Road and back, a distance of 2½ miles.

The race ended in controversy. With valuable prizes on offer, the joy of just taking part rather than the winning was not foremost on every entrant's mind. A gardener, James McLean, won the race but Edmund Went, a shoe smith, immediately objected to the result. He claimed that the winner's wheelbarrow was just a cycle wheel with a box attached. The editor of the Sportsmen adjudicated and disqualified the McLean who promptly said he would not let the matter rest and would take it further. This was far from the sporting ethos or the Corinthian outlook of fair play that many of the middle -classes advocated.[25]

Horticultural excellence

Participation in horticulture by the working-classes was also encouraged. The Ludlow Horticultural Society could not have asked for a more socially exclusive leadership. The Earl of Powis was its president whilst the vice presidents were the Mayor of Ludlow and both members of parliament for the borough.

At each annual show, held in the grounds of the castle, the exhibits were divided into two. Rare and beautiful specimens from the gardens of the nobility and gentry were displayed in one tent whilst the flowers and vegetables of the 'cottagers' could be viewed in a separate one: an example of gardening apartheid.[26]

When the society was founded in 1861, one of its main objects was 'to promote the habits of industry and encourage the better cultivation of flowers, fruit and vegetables.' In a speech opening the 1875 show, by the then-president Alfred Salway of Overton, the hope that participation in horticulture would lead to a change in the habits of the lower orders was articulated more clearly.

'By the cultivation of their gardens, cottagers may do a great deal in adding to their regular income. By taking into the market and selling a portion of their garden produce they might be adding to the material comforts of their respective households and instead of spending their time, as they too often did, in the public house, they would be spending it in their own homes with their families.'

To further encourage the growing of flowers, fruit and vegetables as a leisure pursuit, that year the judges toured the gardens of the working-classes. Out of his own pocket, Salwey awarded five shillings for the best cultivated one in each of the town's four wards.[27]

Boxing in Ludlow

Boxing, in its more disciplined and skilful form, under the regulatory guidance of the British Boxing Board of Control set up in the mid 19th century, took the place of traditional bare knuckle or prize fighting. That form of the sport, as we saw in Chapter One, was once popular in Ludlow but came under increasing pressure to end. As the rules governing the sport evolved and those of the Marquis of Queensbury became accepted, the compulsory use of boxing gloves came into force. In Ludlow the sons of the middle and lower middle-classes now took up the disciplined skill of scientific pugilism. Ludlow Athletic Club, founded in 1882, introduced boxing classes. They ended after a few years but were restarted in 1911 at the Imperial Chambers at the top of Old Street.[28]

After the Great War, the adherents of boxing moved down the social scale. Bouts were held at the Drill Hall organised by the Territorial Army with fighters from Ludlow and the surrounding area. The sport took off locally in 1933 when the British Legion organised a tournament in aid of their local benevolent fund.

The star attraction was a Ludlow man, Tom Pardoe, who was the British Amateur fly weight Champion of

The demand to watch boxing bouts caused the club to move its tournaments from the Drill Hall on Portcullis Lane to the Town Hall after the Second World War. Full houses of 500 spectators were the norm. (Courtesy of Maggie Wright)

Britain 1929-32 and the European Champion of 1931 as well representing Great Britain at the Olympic Games. His fight against a London opponent was supported by a further seven bouts featuring local boxers, and a crowd of 500 came to watch. The result was that the Boys Grammar School organised its own boxing tournament as did the Boy Scouts at their Raven Lane clubroom.

There then followed a district inter-scout troop competition with the boys being divided into eight weight categories. The winning troop received the Kennedy Cup. In addition the Ludlow Amateur Boxing Club, with its headquarters at the New Inn on Upper Galdeford, saw an expansion of its membership that forced them to move their training quarters to the Eagle Hotel on Corve Street and then in 1936 to the Queen's Hotel at Galdeford. The club organised four tournaments a year at the Drill Hall for the remainder of the decade.

Virtually all the boxers had working-class backgrounds: the club had an auctioneer as its chairman, a successful builder as its vice chairman, whilst its treasurer was a councillor and one-time mayor. By 1938 the list of 36 patrons read as a who's who of the local great, the good and the powerful. It was they who donated the many cups and prizes for the contest winners.

Boxing as a sport grew so popular after the Second World War, that bouts were moved to the Town Hall attracting full houses of five hundred spectators. In addition, the patrons, all influential men of the town, were now vice presidents and totalled 52.[29] Boxing in Ludlow had become a successful working-class sport under middle-class guidance.

It is ironic that the sports and leisure clubs that the middle-classes so encouraged the working-classes to join, in order to wean them away from the public houses, set up their headquarters in those self same places. The New Inn on Upper Galdeford was a prime example. Here local boxers once trained and two football teams had their changing rooms. (Courtesy of LHRG Collection)

The local elite also helped in encouraging the formation of a number of working-class clubs and societies. The reason for this was once again the kudos of being seen as generous benefactors but, far more importantly, it was hoped that by encouraging the formation of such clubs, working men would be weaned away from public houses and the leisure pursuits associated with them. The participation in the committee structure of new organisations, the responsibility that this gave, and the need to follow membership rules, was seen as a way of instilling order, pride and respectability. It was believed that these were all attributes that would help men travel along the road to a more sober self-improvement. Ironically, many of these clubs met in public houses. The New Inn on Upper Galdeford was a prime example.

> *'This noted old inn provides accommodation for all kinds of clean sport and recreation, including football, two clubs, Saturday and Thursday teams, two separate dressing rooms with bath and room for referee, angling headquarters, boxing room and room for Amateur Dramatic rehearsals.'*[30]

Pigeon training

The training of homing pigeons, the poor man's racehorses, was very popular and a Ludlow Flying Club was formed in the 1880s to organise local races and enter regional, national and even continental competitions. Its true working-class roots can be seen in its officers. One of its early presidents was Henry Watkins, a journeyman baker, and the vice president Richard Woof, a railway wagon engineer, and the secretary Evan Richards, a bricklayer, supported them.

In 1898, at the annual general meeting held at the Blue Boar public house on Mill Street, the club was renamed the Ludlow Homing Pigeon Society and membership extended to anyone living within eight miles of the Buttercross. The club headquarters then moved to Portcullis Inn on Upper Galdeford.[31]

Pigeon coops in gardens and allotments were a common sight. Owners would be nervously awaiting the arrival of their racing pigeons. No time could be wasted on their arrival for precious minutes could be the difference between winning and losing.
(Courtesy of Patricia Hughes)

The everyday organisation of the society was in the hands of its members with each of them being deemed a committee member with full voting rights. The organisational skills required to run a successful club were quite profound and time-consuming. Weekly arrangements had to made for pigeons to be transported by rail to starting points that were sometimes over a hundred miles away and even as far as the Channel Islands or mainland France. Prior to the introduction of leg rings and clocks in the Edwardian period, register points had to be set up and manned so that owners could run from their lofts when their bird returned to have its tag checked and logged.

Skills were also developed as regards breeding birds for speed, rearing the young and learning the best way to prepare and feed those about to enter a race. Such skills, often kept secret, were then passed down from father to son.

Financial support and the stamp of respectability were gained by having an Honorary President of standing within the community. Someone like Herbert John Allcroft of Stokesay Court provided this. It was he who in 1904 donated a silver cup to be presented to the owner of the winning bird in the annual 122 miles race from Weymouth. Other benefactors provided cups and prizes for the many other races held during most weeks over the summer months. By the interwar years even a

Pigeon racing required meticulous planning. Birds had to be transported to the starting point that could be hundreds of miles away and even abroad. At times Ludlow was the host town and here a staff member at Ludlow Railway Station is releasing pigeons to begin their journey back to their coop and owners.
(Courtesy of LHRG collection)

few of the social elite had become members with Richard De Courcy Peele of Ludford House owning and flying his own birds. The sport's widespread popularity can be seen in that two further clubs were formed: the Ludlow Thursday Flying Club with a membership that tended to be overwhelmingly shopkeepers and shop assistants, and the Ludlow South End Homing Society, with its headquarters at the Barley Mow public house on Lower Broad Street, and whose membership tended to be young and working-class.[32]

Caged birds

In 1907 the Canary and Caged Bird Club was formed, soon to be the Ludlow Caged Bird Society. Its working-class credentials were evidenced by the appointment of Percy Oakes, a plumber and painter, as its first secretary. The club met at the Pheasant Inn where its first treasurer Thomas Sheldon was the publican. Within a year they had successfully organised their first annual show at the Assembly Rooms and invited the Homing Pigeon Society to exhibit their birds as well.[33] As was hoped, organisational and decision-making skills and the shouldering of responsibility, seen by the middle-classes as some of the hallmarks of self-improvement, were being taken on board and honed.

Sunday observance

One further way that the town's social elite attempted to control working-class leisure pursuits was as regards what they could or could not do on a Sunday. Church and Chapel leaders reminded their congregations that, as dictated by the fourth commandment, Sunday was a day for prayer and rest. Since church and chapel attendance was seen as an outward sign of respectability, the middle-classes obeyed, and tried to ensure that the working-classes did likewise. However, it is ironic that the first crack in the wall of Sunday observance came at a committee made up of middle-class councillors. This was the town's Attractions Committee that had just purchased rowing boats for hire on the River Teme, and it was they who allowed their boats to be hired on a Sunday.

It should perhaps be noted here that the bulk of the committee were the most important tradesmen of the town and their instinct was to attract as many visitors to Ludlow as possible, since increased visitor numbers brought increased trade that in turn brought increased profit. It appears that in this case the love of Mammon held the greater sway in their

The first crack in the ban on leisure activities in Ludlow on a Sunday came when the Attractions Committee purchased rowing boats for hire in 1905. Here the new boats are being 'christened' which is rather ironic since it was leading members of both church and chapel who opposed such secular activities on what they saw as a holy day of rest. However, it was still banned in 1938 on the waters above Dinham weir due to the views of the Earl of Plymouth.

decision. But it was not for long. Within a few months the decision was reversed as both church and chapel exerted pressure.

The next crack in the Sunday Observance Laws came with the decision of Ludlow Golf Club to allow members to play on Sundays when the club re-opened after the Great War. The reason for their decision was probably because the local aristocracy and gentry had always been an important section of the club in the nineteenth century and were still influential at the start of the twentieth. This group had always been far more liberal in their views about church teaching than the new urban middle-classes that had grown with the Industrial Revolution and become imbued with the ethos of Victorian respectability.

This movement towards a different approach by some to Sunday leisure habits came to the fore in 1923 but was beaten off. The tennis section of the Burway Cricket, Tennis, Bowls and Hockey Club asked to be able to use the courts on a Sunday. At a special general meeting this was refused after members of the other sections of the club threatened resignations. In the same year, the Town Council refused a request that council playing fields be opened for games on Sunday afternoons. An editorial in the Ludlow Advertiser highlighted some of the bitterness felt in the town against the influential few ignoring the wishes of the many. It saw the refusal to open the playing fields as the punishment of a class: golf could be played on a Sunday by the upper classes but not football by the working-classes. The editorial went on to say that:

> *'The question of Sabbath Observance is surrounded by so much cant and hypocrisy that it becomes almost impossible to get it discussed and decided without engendering heat and wounding some peoples susceptibilities. We could cite the case of an individual who, whilst making himself conspicuous in opposing Sunday Games in public, was known to play clock golf on his private lawn on Sunday afternoons.'*[34]

up to cover the summer months of 1941. This decision flew in the face of evidence presented by both the Army Welfare Officer and the local police, who pointed out that the cinemas were packed each Sunday and that it was far better to have all these people inside enjoying themselves rather that wandering the streets and congregating in shop doorways.[38]

Unsurprisingly, the pressure on the magistrates to refuse a licence came from the leaders and congregations of both church and chapel, whose representatives argued that not only was Sunday the Lord's Day but that the cinema, predominantly watched by a working-class audience at the time, perverted the morals of young people and would lead to an increase in delinquency. One nonconformist minister reminded the bench that they too had believed this when recently sentencing two young men for theft. Part of the punishment they dictated was that the youths would be banned from attending the cinema for two years. Evidence of the depth of feeling that the question engendered can be discerned when the Rector of St Laurence's went as far as describing Sunday cinema as 'a thing of evil' and protested, 'If people want to be Godless, why don't they go to Germany or Russia?'

It was only when a petition by war workers, who had been sent to the town by the Government, was added to the pleas of the armed forces and the police, that the magistrates, by the narrowest majority of just one, renewed the licence for the winter of 1941/42. From that point on Sunday cinema was in Ludlow for good though an attempt to stop it was only narrowly defeated after the war ended.[39]

Such efforts to mould working-class leisure habits were not the only external influences at work. As will be seen in the following chapter, a number of leisure pursuits that began as catering only for the middle-classes, slowly evolved to encompass adherents from further down the social scale.

CHAPTER 4

Upper and Middle-Class Leisure

Though a number of blood sports enjoyed by the upper classes were banned in the 19th century, as was seen in chapter one, most of the traditional rural pursuits of hunting, shooting and coursing remained untouched. In addition, they could still enjoy horse racing and they even found time to carry on playing cricket and to take up fresh sports such as polo, golf, tennis and curling.

Returning military officers imported polo into Britain from India in the 1860s and in 1874 the Hurlingham Polo Association became the United Kingdom's governing body and drew up the first British rules. It was 1892 when a club was formed in Ludlow with its playing ground on the racecourse at Bromfield. The Right Honourable Lord Windsor was appointed president and the secretary was W. Howard of Broncroft Castle. As well as playing matches against neighbouring teams such as Worcestershire, sports days or gymkhanas became an annual event in the social calendar. Here could be seen the local aristocracy and gentry at play, dropping potatoes into a bucket at the gallop, riding whilst balancing an egg in a spoon, and galloping to a line of boxes, dismounting and then dressing properly in whatever ladies garment was found inside the one they chose to open. Suitably attired, the rider then remounted to finish the race. Amongst the glitterati in attendance at the club's first sports day in Ludford Park were the Charltons of Caynham Court, the McMickings of Culmington Manor, the Sitwells of Ferney Hall, the Broughton Knights of Downton Castle and the Kevill Davies of Croft Castle. Further years of enjoyment followed and at one point the club moved to Oakley Park, but it never really put down firm roots and had disappeared by 1909 when its pavilion was sold to the newly formed Bowls Club on the Burway.[1] The game was revived in 1936 when a new Ludlow Polo Club was formed. The first game was played on a field at Elsich against North Staffordshire. Most of the team were military men from county families including Captain Kennard, Captain E. H. Rouse-Boughton and a Major Darby.[2]

Another even shorter-lived sport, was curling. Edward V11, when Prince of Wales, became the patron of the Royal Caledonian Curling Club and retained that position when he became King. With the royal connection, curling became fashionable with the aristocracy and as a result a club was formed locally during the winter of 1906/07 with the Earl of Plymouth as president. A rink was constructed at Bromfield, near to the racecourse, probably using one of the frozen pools at the gravel pits on the site of the old Roman Camp. This sport seems to have disappeared by the outbreak of the Great War in 1914.

Golf, also taken up, did survive though later was to be diluted as regards the social make up of its membership. Ludlow Golf Club was formed at the racecourse at Bromfield in 1889 and originally had just nine holes. Its initial membership was limited to members of the aristocracy, gentry, church and the professions, only numbering one hundred by 1912. The social background of the team members who played Shrewsbury in 1892 is evidence of this: two churchmen, together with Sitwell of Henley Hall, McMiching of Delbury Hall and a Colonel Spilling. This narrow membership is further illuminated in 1919 when the Mayor of Ludlow, Alderman Sheldon, called a meeting to discuss the possibility of opening a new Ludlow Borough Golf Club with a course on Whitcliffe that would be open to anyone who could afford the annual subscription. This solution was offered due to the complaint that the existing golf club was:

> *'always a very exclusive institution, membership being confined to the gentry and professional classes; indeed it was only in very recent years that entrance was granted to a very limited number of gentlemen who had 'soiled their hands' in trade and this after numerous attempts to broaden the basis of the club had been turned down.'*

It was claimed that by 1914 only a few townsmen had been 'fortunate to squeeze through the club's portals.'[3] The proposed new club did not come to fruition but it appears that it did encourage Ludlow Golf Club to widen the basis of its membership to the town's middle classes though the members still drew the line at those further down the social scale. When the course re-opened in 1919, after it had been partly ploughed up to help feed the nation during the Great War, it was decided to extend it to eighteen holes and this came to fruition in 1923. The impetus for this, it was said, was due to a 'considerable increase in membership over the last two years.'[4]

One way the upper classes were more liberal in outlook was in their attitude to the participation of women in sport. Women had always ridden to the Hunt and they played golf in Ludlow from the very beginning though, admittedly, not always enjoying the same club facilities as the men. When the very first Ladies Competition was held in 1900, the women had to use separate quarters. Space was made available to them in the Race Course Grandstand where they could keep their clubs and have lunch separate from the male membership.[5]

Archery, in the form of the Archers of the Teme, had been a leisure pursuit for the upper classes since the club was formed in 1857 by Lady Curtis of Caynham Court, and one in which women played an equal part. The members initially met six times a year on Ludlow Castle Green though this number increased and they also met elsewhere on occasions such as when they were invited by Sir William and Lady Millman of Moor Park to hold an archery contest in their grounds. Membership that was initially set at eighty was always decided by ballot. It increased to 150 by 1867 later rising to 160. Records of individual scores, listed in local newspapers, showed that women made up about two thirds of the competitors with most, though not all, being single. As for the men, churchmen made up a significant proportion. This exclusive club still met to shoot in the castle grounds until it was disbanded shortly before 1930.[6]

The local upper classes appear to have taken up club cricket quite early and there is evidence that Ludlow had a cricket team as early as 1831, who played on the Old Field at Bromfield. A fresh club was formed in 1845 that had 64 members and played matches at Ludford, afterwards sitting 'down to a sumptuous repast at the *Charlton Arms*.' Their social background is seen in that all the members were described as 'gentlemen.' The club collapsed in 1860 but was resurrected two years later when the ground moved to Fishmore Road before moving back to the Old Field at Bromfield.[7] By 1885 the club had moved yet again this time to its permanent home at Burway Lane where they had a 'comfortable pavilion.'

Dissatisfaction with the influence that the upper-class members still wielded, as regards the running of the club and the team selection, surfaced in 1890. In a letter to the *Ludlow Advertiser*, a few of the older players wrote that whilst 'we fully recognise the support given to the club by the gentlemen of the neighbourhood and their friends when staying with them, we feel that such friends should not be

The Archers of the Teme, formed in 1857, met in Ludlow Castle grounds until well into the interwar years. Its membership was always exclusive and unlike many leisure pursuits the majority of participants were female. (Courtesy of Shropshire Museum Service)

picked in place of regular local players.' The result was that at that year's AGM a compromise solution was agreed. The chairman and team captain, Francis Sitwell of Ferney Hall, who was an Oxford Blue, argued that in order to maximise subscriptions from patrons, and to have a strong enough team to continue their fixtures against teams such as the MCC, the club had to remain a 'town and country club.' The continued need for solid financial support was partly required due to the fact that the club employed two professional cricketers each year. One that hailed from Nottinghamshire in 1892 was paid 80/- a week, four times the average local wage. A decision was

Thanks to having extensive playing fields, unlike the town's elementary schools that the bulk of the Ludlow's children attended, cricket was one sport the Boy's Grammar School played. It was also one of the reasons why Ludlow Cricket Club still remained mainly a middle class bastion until the Second World War.

(Courtesy of Shropshire Museum Service)

thus made to have two teams with separate fixture lists. The main team would draw players from all over South Shropshire whilst the other would contain mainly players from Ludlow.[8]

Change still remained very slow as regards the social makeup of the club as evidenced by their officers in 1905. Lord Windsor was president whilst Francis Sitwell of Ferney Hall was the first team captain with the Reverend Hugh Hastings, a schoolmaster at the Grammar School, as his vice-captain. The second team captain was William Marston, a Ludlow Corn Merchant, who had yet another churchman, the Reverend Wolfendon, as his vice-captain.[9] However, this did help as regards the participation of women in the game. A Ladies team first played in 1909 and the matches proved very popular and 'a great attraction.' The star player was the eighteen-year-old Marjorie Keysell, the daughter of a retired Ludlow wine merchant.

In the villages, with their smaller pool of talent to choose from, teams were more socially mixed though this sometimes led to the gentlemanly rules of fair play to be ignored. In 1912, the Bitterley team were accused by their opponents of 'a lack of sporting spirit'. They claimed that Bitterley had deleted three names in the scorebook after the match had started and replaced them with those of better players. To rub salt into the wound, it appears those players were not even club members. In Ludlow, cricket was also being played by all classes, with a team of Ludlow Tradesmen playing a team of Licenced Victuallers on the Burway ground.[10] Working-class participation in the game accelerated when cricket was introduced into the elementary schools in the early Edwardian years.

After the Great War, Ludlow Cricket Club actively encouraged players of talent from all classes to join and play. In order to do this they began an evening limited-overs knockout competition in 1925. The teams that entered included the Hockey Club, Bankers, Tradesmen, Post Office, Civil Servants, Corn Merchants, and the Auctioneers. The Railwaymen soon joined them, and reached the final in 1929. To this growing mix two teams of Ladies were added in 1930. Though critics saw the competition 'as an attempt to injure legitimate cricket,' the counter argument was that it successfully fostered local interest in the game and discovered local talent. Though it was admitted that this limited overs cricket was 'less dignified and skilful than the more orthodox form' it was pointed out that 'it seems to possess immense power of attraction and large crowds attend all matches' providing a financial boost to the club.[11] From being a game for the gentry and upper middle classes, local cricket was now a game for all, though by the outbreak of the Second World War, Ludlow Cricket Club itself still retained a middle-class bias as its main source of members were ex-grammar school boys.

A Ludlow Boating Club was in existence in 1834 when it took part in a competition against Worcester Rowing Club on waters between Stourport and Bewdley. With the permission of Lord Windsor the club could use the upper waters of the River Teme above Dinham Weir, and had a boathouse on one bank. In thanks, Lord Windsor was presented with

Middle class women also rowed and, as here, even took part in races during the annual regattas held on the River Teme during the Edwardian years. (Courtesy of Shropshire Museum Sevice)

boxed silver oars on the occasion of his marriage in 1883. A year later, on the birth of his son and heir, a Union Jack was raised above the boathouse and a huge bonfire lit in celebration. The club's narrow membership can be discerned from the owners of the four gigs (two oarsmen and a cox) that raced in 1884. They were *Waterworld*, owned by Llwellyn Jones, a solicitor; *Rose*, owned by Samuel Valentine, a high class grocer; *Lizzie*, owned by George Wells, a bank manager; and *Marie*, owned by Arthur Marston, another solicitor and the club's chairman. In 1905 the membership was still being described as 'select rather than numerous.'[12]

Also using the river for leisure purposes was the Ludlow Bathing Club, founded in 1867, which used the waters between Dinham and Mill Street weirs. By 1894 a Ladies Bathing Club was also in existence. For modesty, whilst changing before and

after swimming, they erected a bathing house in the orchard at the bottom of Lower Mill Street. A few years later they erected a second one on the same town bank.[13] Unlike the Boating Club, the Bathing Club welcomed those in the tradesmen class as members. The club's first chairman was Herbert Grieves, a dispensing chemist, whilst the men who took part in the first 150 yards swimming race included a draper's assistant, a trainee accountant, and an ironmonger's assistant. From the start, bathing dress had to modest and 'in accordance with rules of the club the competitors wore drawers of the true acrobatic cut' that went down to the knees and covered the upper body.[14]

Ludlow Swimming club, using the River Teme, began playing water polo matches from the 1890s. In the early years of the twentieth century, when they held their annual sports day in conjunction with the regatta, members put on exhibition games to entertain the spectators. (Courtesy of Shropshire Museum Services)

In 1885 the club was renamed the Ludlow Swimming Club and all members still had to wear uniform bathing dress. Annual races and aquatic sports were held and the sports included a greasy pole event and the long dive where, once in the water with the head immersed, no part of the body could move and only the impetus of the dive could propel you forward. Later, to attract larger crowds to the sports day, other fun events were devised such as the Old Clothes Race and the Duck Hunt. In the former, swimmers had to wear a jacket, waistcoat and trousers to swim across the river and back to win 5/-. In the latter game, a swimmer with a bell attached had to evade blindfolded hunters for five minutes in order to win 5/-.[15] After being successfully incorporated in the annual sports day events, in the 1890s a water polo section was set up with its own committee which then developed a fixture list with games arranged with Shrewsbury and Hereford amongst others.

After the Great War the club had 179 members of whom 43 were ladies, and the annual sports days were reinstated. Though it then soon collapsed it was reformed under the auspices of the Ludlow Athletic Club and an annual swimming gala was again enjoyed.[16]

Fishing was a pastime enjoyed by all, but such fishing was limited to the Whitcliffe bank of the river below Dinham Bridge, To fish elsewhere required permission from the landowner. In 1900, Dr Lang, taking advantage of his friendship with the manager of the Oakley Hall Estate, managed to obtain permission for ten men to fish the waters for three quarters of a mile above the boathouse that was situated upstream from Dinham weir. As a result, the Ludlow Angling Society was formed in 1900 with its headquarters at the *New Inn* on Upper Galdeford. The initial membership was Dr Lang and nine of his invited friends. They included two more from the medical profession, one churchman, a retired schoolmaster, a retired actor, a retired miller as well as the landlord of the *New Inn*. If

The Ludlow Angling Society, given sole permission to fish the waters above Dinham Weir by the Oakley Estate, was made up of a small, select group of middle class men. Here in 1908, William Perry, the landlord of the New Inn where the society had its headquarters, stands proudly with his catch that he caught in just two hours. (Courtesy of Shropshire Museum Services)

The members of the other two bowls clubs, at the Burway and the Castle club on the Linney, also tended to have mainly middle class membership. The Burway Club allowed women to play before the First World War though at the Castle Club their acceptance was rather slower for as Archdeacon Maude remarked in 1920 though they did not play bowls the ladies were very good in 'helping them with the teas'. (Courtesy of Shropshire Museum Services)

a member died then the other members chose a replacement. This elite group, whose membership had increased to just fifteen by 1936 to match the extra rods allowed by the Earl of Plymouth, also managed to negotiate extra fishing rights to a section of the River Corve from the Bromfield Road Bridge to its confluence with the Teme. To bring in further finance to keep the waters restocked a new angling club was set up to fish this new section of local water. This was called the Corve Fishing Club and set up its headquarters at the *Rose and Crown* public house. This too was limited in membership with a maximum of twenty, though it was possible to obtain a small number of 2d day tickets.[17]

Bowls was another long established game for the gentry taken up by the middle classes. In the mid nineteenth century, there was only one bowls club in Ludlow and that was the Whitcliffe Bowls Club situated at the *Ludlow Arms* (later the *Bowling Green Hotel*), an old established inn on the Whitcliffe Road. It was played at first by the local gentry who also used the fives court there after leaving their original court next to Mortimer's Tower in Ludlow Castle. By 1850, however, new bowling members were more likely to earn their living in the commercial sphere. In the second half of the 19th century it was quite usual to find Ludlow's mayor and a number of aldermen and councillors on the organising committee. By the early 20th century it still had

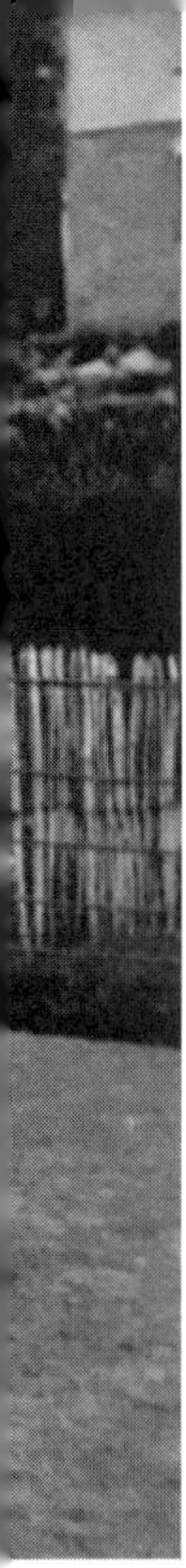

In the nineteenth century, as this long-lost garden where the Market Square car park is now situated shows, croquet was the main game enjoyed by the middle classes at home. However, by the 1890s this had been replaced by lawn tennis where mixed doubles allowed chaperoned courtship rituals to take place.

some support of the local gentry and aristocracy, and the Earl of Plymouth paid for the replacement green in 1908 but players were now of the tradesman class. Four Ludlow men were in the County team in 1913 and they epitomised the local players of the time: Edward Harding, a draper, William Parsonage, a commission agent, Clement Bodenham, house furnisher, and John Paterson, timber merchant.[18]

By 1914 two other clubs had set down roots and both were solidly middle class. One was attached to the Ludlow Cricket Club and in 1911 its captain was Edward Wood, a man of private means. Ladies were allowed to play here and the two finalists in the mixed doubles in 1912 were Mildred Evan, the daughter of the landlord of the *Unicorn Inn* on Lower Corve Street, and Mrs Marsh Gwillim, the wife of the District Surveyor. The second club was the Castle Bowls Club attached to the Tennis Club on the Linney. Again middle class in character, women had less of a role even in 1920. As the Venerable Archdeacon Maude explained at that year's annual dinner held at the Bull Hotel, ladies played tennis but not bowls. However, 'they had the pleasure of meeting them when they came to have tea and the ladies were also very kind in helping them with the teas.'[19]

Socially the game began to change in the interwar years partly due to the efforts of Canon Cheshire of Bromfield who set up a Ludlow and District Bowls League. Village teams, with their greater social mix, and teams such as the railwaymen now played and opened the way for all classes to play the game, though the three Ludlow teams still tended to retain their middle-class bias until after the Second World War.[20]

The birth of lawn tennis in the late 19th century saw the formation of the Ludlow Castle Lawn Tennis Club at the Linney and a second one attached to the cricket club at Burway Lane. The social makeup of both clubs was solidly of the gentry and upper middle classes and this can be seen in a joint tournament held in 1900. The four men who organised it

Whitcliffe Bowls Club, that played at the *Ludlow Arms* on Whitcliffe (often known as the *Bowling Green Hotel*) was the oldest club in Ludlow. The local gentry began it, though by the second half of the nineteenth century the membership was solidly middle class, as this group photograph shows. (Courtesy of Shropshire Museum Services)

were Willoughby Sitwell of Ferney Hall who was an ex cavalry officer, Edward Leake, a Ludlow gentleman of private means, Tilsey Price, described as a student of the arts, and Robert Marston a local solicitor. Of the thirty-two men who took part in the tournament not one tradesman can be discerned. All were from the professional classes of Ludlow (Law, Medicine etc.) or men who had their own private income, whilst those from the surrounding district were landowners, ex army officers or churchmen. Women were not excluded and could be found playing, though at first just in the mixed doubles. They all tended to be single and they too were from families not associated with trade.[21]

Hockey was another sport played by the middle classes and one in which women could also take part. Initially two separate clubs, a mixed team was playing by 1903. (Courtesy of Roger Furniss)

This initial social exclusion was short-lived becoming outdated by the Edwardian years as tennis was soon taken up with alacrity by the middle classes, as it could be played on the extensive lawns behind their newly built villas often replacing the croquet sets. It was a game that could be enjoyed socially between friends and neighbours and a game in which the middle-aged could take part when the sports of their youth grew too exhausting. Mixed doubles could also be played in a suitably chaperoned environment and become part of a safe setting for the courtship ritual. As well as increasing and broadening the membership of the two tennis clubs, Edwardian Ludlow saw a popular annual tournament being held in the grounds of Overmead House off Livesey Road, the home of Samuel Valentine who owned a high-class grocery shop on Broad Street. After 1920 Ludlow Castle Tennis Club also allowed the pupils of the Girls High School the use of their courts. Tennis had become a pursuit of the entire middle-class spectrum. To cater for this increase in membership, by 1928 the Burway Club had six grass courts and two hard courts.[22] Alongside this increase came a widening of the opportunities for women to play. Throughout the 1920s, in addition to mixed doubles, ladies singles matches, as well as ladies doubles, were to be seen in tournaments and by 1930, at the Burway Club, they played their own matches against other local clubs such as Tenbury.[23] Women were also members of the Ludlow Badminton Club that played at the roller skating rink on Lower Broad Street. Their matches against clubs such as Tenbury, Church Stretton and Hereford were all mixed doubles.[24]

It was seen in chapter three how the working classes were introduced to association football in an attempt to instil physical fitness, team spirit, gentlemanly sporting conduct and a respect for rules. This was successful in that the game became very popular, but less successful as regards aspects of perceived correct character building. One result was that middle-class youth chose to retreat to new sporting pastimes. Tennis was not the only sport chosen, for hockey was yet another example of a middle-class retreat from the new sporting habits of the main populace.

Ludlow Hockey Club, formed in 1896, became and remained a middle-class bastion. Their first home match, played against Leominster, is thought to have taken place on the Grammar School football pitch that was then situated in Ludford Park. The game was followed by tea at the *Charlton Arms Hotel*.[25] By 1898 the club had moved to the cricket ground at the Burway that became its permanent home. The club had an unstable beginning due to a dearth of players and had to be resurrected in 1907. Its middle-class membership can be seen in the make-up of its officers, with the captain being a man of private means who was replaced by a bank clerk, whilst the president Charles Keysell was a wine merchant. This club too gave middle-class women the opportunity to participate in

In 1913 hockey replaced football during the Spring Term and helped the town team membership in the years to come. These young men were photographed on the cusp of the First World War. The player at the bottom right, Harold Mellings from Bromfield, was to become a flying ace with 15 kills to his credit before being killed in action himself in July 1918 aged just eighteen.
(Courtesy of Robert Burns)

sport. The sexes were initially separated into two clubs sharing the same facilities and in 1901 the ladies became affiliated to the All England Women's Hockey Association. However, the clubs were turning out a mixed eleven for some matches by 1903. When hockey restarted after a pause during the Great War, the two separate clubs became one though this had to resuscitated in 1924 after it fell on difficult times once more. The club's survival, until the late 1930s, was helped by the fact that the Girls High School took up the sport. Hockey at the Boys' Grammar School had already replaced football during the spring term of 1913.[26]

One reason for the dearth of working-class girls participating in local sport was due to their schooling. When plans were made to instil team spirit and introduce a keep-fit programme amongst munition girls during the First World War, by encouraging team games, it was discovered that they had never had the opportunity to play any. Unlike girl's public schools and high schools, elementary Schools, including those in Ludlow, had not offered team sports to girls, only physical training drills.[27]

Rugby Union was another game that became a middle-class refuge. Andrew Cecil Telfer, appointed headmaster of the Boys' Grammar School in 1927, in an attempt to resurrect the public school image that it had held in the previous century,

Virtually all these Ludlow Rugby Club players in 1934, the year that the club was formed, were old boys of the local Grammar School. The School remained the main source for playing members for many years. (Courtesy of Claire Powick Hainsworth)

replaced association football as a school sport with rugby union, As a result, in 1934 the Ludlow Rugby Football Club was founded. It played for most of its first twenty years on a pitch next to the school ground off Bromfield Road, and the membership was almost exclusively made up of old boys of the grammar school and remained so for many years to come.[28]

Athletic prowess in the form of running was also introduced into public and grammar schools and therefore experienced by the sons of Ludlow's middle classes. The paper chase, or fox and hounds or hare and hounds as it was variously called, could often be seen locally. Hare and Hounds was part of the sporting calendar of Ludlow Grammar School, usually enjoyed during the winter months. Two boys, the hares, laid a trail of paper for the remaining boys, the hounds, to follow and attempt to catch them.

On one chase the hares ran to Fishmore, past the rifle butts, on to Downton Hall, back over Haytons Bent and then towards Stanton Lacy where they were finally overtaken and caught. The Ludlow Harriers, formed in the late 1880s as a section of the Gymnastics Club, carried on the sport interspersed with their usual long-distance running. In one such race the two 'foxes' chased by six 'hounds' set off from Old Street, ran over Whitcliffe to Priors Halton, then on to the racecourse and from there back to Ludlow. The seven minutes between the two starting off times was not narrowed. The local Boy Scout troop also enjoyed this type of race in the years just prior to the Great War.[29]

The view of athletic competition for its own sake was what lay behind the formation of the Ludlow Amateur Athletic Club in 1882, just two years after the birth of the national Amateur Athletic Association that set down a single set of rules. Two sports days were held in the first year: at Easter and in August. In addition to the foot races over 120, 200 and 400 yards, there was a hurdle race, a mile race, and a tug of war competition. To further entertain the spectators a 440 yard obstacle race was held where amongst other things competitors had to crawl through barrels, jump hurdles and navigate under a pole 9' above the ground. In 1898, the members voted to amalgamate with the Ludlow and District Cycle Club who had a very similar middle and lower middle-class membership mainly due to the cost of purchasing a cycle.[30] Held on the Castle Green, the sports days now included a half-mile cycle race and a tortoise race where the slowest cyclist won. After such sports days in the early Edwardian years ended, they were re-introduced on Easter Monday 1912 when one was held on the Mill Street sports ground along the bank of the River Teme. All social classes were encouraged to take part and this resulted in over 220 entries, and in addition, all local elementary schools were invited to take part. The day attracted over one thousand paying spectators. It also included a long-distance race that started in Clee Hill village and ended at the sports ground.[31]

The bicycle or velocipede craze came to Ludlow in 1869. As part of their sales promotion, Messrs Prinn and Dale, a shop situated on the High Street, hired a professional rider to teach purchasers how to ride. This was carried out in a warehouse adjacent to the Rose and Crown Inn and twenty learners attended the first session.

The Ludlow Cycle Club was formed that year though by 1891 it still had only 33 members and its middle-class credentials were still in evidence as the president was then a churchman, its captain a stationer and printer, and its secretary a bookseller. In 1895, in an attempt to increase its membership the club became the Ludlow and District Cycle Club. Also, thanks to mass production and the invention of the inflatable tyre, cycling not only became cheaper but more comfortable and safe. Outings in the 1890s became more adventurous. Two were held each week, the first on Thursdays; that was Ludlow's early closing day and allowed shopkeepers and shop workers to participate; and Saturdays. Places such as Newnham Bridge,

Aston-on-Clun and Knighton were cycled to with return distances of between 12 to 48 miles being usual. One outing to Wellington, however, was of 82 miles.[32]

Cycling was enjoyed by both sexes though for ladies it was more a social activity that an athletic or endurance one. In 1898 there was a proposal for a separate Ladies Cycle Club though nothing appears to have come of it, though in the following year the Wesley Guild Cycle Club was formed. This was a social cycling club for both ladies and gentlemen. 'Scorching' or riding fast was not allowed and a pace was always set to accommodate 'timid' riders. Gentle rides out to villages often included attending a religious service in a local chapel.[33]

Athletic competition was nearly always to be seen as part of the days programme at fetes and galas from the nineteenth century. As the belief in the virtues of physical fitness gained ground, from1925 all local elementary schoolchildren, both boys and girls, were invited to attend an annual athletic sports day within the Castle grounds. (Courtesy of Shropshire Museum Service)

As cycling grew more and more popular and widespread, the freedom that cycling gave to young people outside of any organised club activity was described in detail in a newspaper article. Two male friends set off on their cycles from Ludlow at 10.45 on a Sunday morning and made their way to Church Stretton, enjoying the sights along the way, where they met, by agreement, a compatriot who was a non-cyclist who had made the same journey by train. After lunch at a local hotel, where they left the bicycles, the trio then set off on a ramble that took in Caradoc Hill and the Long Mynd before returning to enable their friend to catch the 5.30pm train. After collecting their cycles from the hotel the two of them rode back to Ludlow arriving about 9pm.[34]

One result of cycling's growing popularity was what became an annual Fancy Dress Parade raising funds for local charities. The first was held in 1895 and raised money for the Cottage Hospital and the Dispensary. Held on a Thursday evening in late October and organised by a grocer's clerk, a grocer's assistant and a solicitor's clerk, the procession toured the streets of Ludlow. Starting at their headquarters at the *Queen's Head*, Galdeford, the torchlight procession travelled along Tower Street, High Street, Castle Square, Mill Street, Bell Lane, Broad Street and back to Corve Street and Old Street before returning to the *Queen's Head* where a cold supper awaited. The Parade was led by the town's fire engine and firemen, and followed by St George's Football Club, the Ludlow Town Band, the Church of England Temperance Drum and Fife Band and then forty cyclists in fancy dress. A soldier, sailor, clown jockey, butcher, Buffalo Bill, a Spanish gentleman and Kings and Queens, amongst many other characters, could be seen. The streets were thronged with onlookers and a dozen people walked among them collecting charitable donations. 'For picturesque effect it was undoubtedly the best local procession seen in Ludlow for many year *(sic)*' Each year until 1900 saw the event being staged and organised by the Cycling and Athletic Club. When it was resurrected in 1905, under fresh management, the club was invited to take its place once more.[35]

Bicycles got progressively cheaper during the interwar years and, allied to the fact that it became possible to buy one on hire purchase, with the cost spread over many weeks, it meant that they were affordable to the working classes. By 1920 cycling was becoming no longer limited mainly to the middle classes, albeit the lower middle classes. In that year,

When the Ludlow Cycle Club was first formed in 1891 it had a middle class membership due to the early expensive cost of bicycles. At first the cycles were used very much as horses with various cavalry skills being practised such as bending down at speed to pick up objects, in this case a small dummy, and hooking rings.
(Courtesy of Shropshire Museum Service)

As with many middle class sports, ladies participated in the new cycling craze. Here at the Castle Bowls and Tennis Club on the Linney, a lady rider, despite the encumbrance of her dress, is lancing rings. (Courtesy of Lottie James)

385,000 bicycles were sold nationally, but this rose to 1.61 million by 1935. By this date owning a bicycle had become almost a rite of passage for teenage boys, though less so for working class girls as domestic and moral shackles kept many locked to the home. The result was that the interwar years saw the heyday of cycling the lanes and byways of the countryside for pleasure. Cycling had become, not only an efficient mode of travel that allowed an easier trip to school or work, but also a widespread leisure pursuit.

As bicycles became commonplace the more adventurous of the middle classes turned to motorcycles, forming the Ludlow and District Motor Cycle Club in 1919 with Herbert Grant, a tobacconist on the High Street as the main organising force. Initially the club had a membership of nearly thirty. A first, a rather sedate trial outing was held, starting from their headquarters at the *Feathers Hotel*, and lasting two hours with a maximum speed limit of 20 mph. A typical Sunday ride was when twenty-three members set out to Llandrindod where they had a picnic and enjoyed an impromptu hill climb on the way. Shortly afterwards the club reformed as the Ludlow and District Motor Cycle and Light Car Club and now met at the *Queens Head* on Galdeford. They rode out to different venues each Sunday for social gatherings.

They also took part in organised, timed hill climbs. At one, at Limekilns Bank, The Hope, a large crowd watched entrants from Ludlow, Kidderminster, Leominster and

As the cost of owning a bicycle fell around the turn of the twentieth century, membership of the Ludlow and District Cycle Club moved down the social scale as can be seen in this group photograph of the Ludlow and District Cycle Club.
(Courtesy of Shropshire Museum Service)

In the interwar years motorcycle outings became popular and the Ludlow and District Motor Cycle Club was formed. Sidecars allowed wives and friends to join the riders on trips into the countryside often followed by a picnic. (Courtesy of LHRG Archive)

Wellington compete. As motorcycle and car ownership grew in Ludlow the club could drop District from its name in 1927.[36]

The growing popularity of this type of transport for competitive enjoyment saw a Motor Gymkhana being held in 1930, organised by the YMCA, just off the Bromfield Road. A crowd of 700 watched motorcycle events including an egg and spoon race, riding the plank, and musical chairs with a female pillion rider. For motorcars, among many other amusements for the spectators to enjoy, were a tortoise race, a reverse race and an obstacle race.[37]

But as the ownership of motorcycles moved down the social scale, the middle classes, in their quest for social exclusivity, now took to the motorcar, forming the Ludlow and District Motor Club in 1932 though some members still owned and competed with motorbikes. The club, as befitted the social standing of its members, had its early headquarters at the *Feathers Hotel*, though they soon moved to the equally prestigious *Angel Hotel* on Broad Street. Treasure hunts became their main social activity, often followed by a dance in the *Angel Hotel's* Nelson Room. To ensure a staggered start, treasure hunts often began with a foot race to collect the first clue. The middle-class membership can be discerned in that one hunt was won by a Dr and Mrs Zair, whilst it is interesting to note that in second place both the driver and co-driver were women: Mrs Estyn-Jones, a solicitor's wife, and a Mrs Bendall. This is yet another example of middle-class women having the time and opportunity, unlike their working-class

As the years passed motorcycling became available to a wider section of the populace especially young men and more adventurous hill climbing was enjoyed. This group, c1950, are on the Whitcliffe. (Courtesy of Shropshire Museum Service)

After the First World War motorcars became more available to the town's middle classes. A Motor Club was set up and Treasure Hunts planned. But motoring did not have to be organised and drives out into the countryside became a popular leisure pursuit for those fortunate enough to be able to afford a car.

(Courtesy of Paul Lenton)

counterparts, to participate in competitive leisure activities. Motor Club members also had the time and the money to take part in long distance trials such as that from London to Lands End in which four Ludlow drivers, including two solicitors, won awards. A few weeks later, this very active club entered ten cars in the London to Exeter trial. One member, the son of the Vicar of Stanton Lacy, even took his motorbike to Bavaria in 1935 to take part in a rally.[38]

Walking for leisure had also become a very popular recreational activity for many people by the end of the nineteenth century. In 1897, at Church Stretton station, the arrival of the 5.30pm train was described in awe.

> *'Our surprise was great when between two and three hundred passengers emerged – the fair sex, mind you, predominantly – from the train. On enquiry we found that this was quite an ordinary*

occurrence during the summer months … Half an hour later the streets were deserted; everyone had taken to the footpaths leading to the hills, till 9.30 when the mail train will take them back.'[39]

By the interwar years, rambling and hiking had become part of a craze for healthy outdoor recreation. There was, however, a clear social distinction between the two. Ramblers tended to be middle class and educated, with an interest in the topography and natural history of the countryside. The men tended to be seen in knee breeches, long woollen socks and tailored jackets. A Rambling Club was set up in Ludlow in 1930 at the *Greyhound Inn* situated at the start of Gravel Hill. This organised weekly rambles and a field day once a month. Hikers, often of skilled working and lower middle-class origins, imbued with a desire for self-improvement, tended to wear shorts, shirts and boots that were often ex-army.[40] Hiking was also one of the few occasions where men and women could share equally in a recreational activity, and this at a time when separate spheres dictated differing roles for the sexes in the home environment.

The growth of the popular activities of hiking and cycling, was aided by the rapid expansion of the Youth Hostel Movement from 1930, offering rooms for 1/- a night and putting the opportunity of a cheap holiday within the reach of thousands. In 1932 a hostel was opened in Ludlow at 112 Corve Street. As well as being able to sleep forty people, it had

Day outings to places like Church Stretton by rail in order to walk on the Shropshire Hills was enjoyed by many especially the middle and lower middle classes. This expectant family group await a train on Ludlow station. (Courtesy of Lottie James)

a common room and a communal kitchen, though guests had to provide their own cutlery and crockery. Membership costs were kept low being 2/6d per annum for the under twenty fives and 5/- for all others. It was noted locally that 'in these

A walk followed by a picnic was one leisure pursuit that ladies such as these could participate in together, especially those belonging to the middle classes who had servants to carry out the drudgery of housework. (Courtesy of Shropshire Museum Service)

days, when there are so many hikers, hostels will supply a long-felt need, I should say, for there is certainly need of good clean accommodation to meet the pockets of the majority of the working class who love the country.' Hiking for others could just be a single day's experience. Many would come by train to Ludlow to explore both the town and the surrounding countryside, walking an average of between five to eight miles before re-boarding the train to return home.[41]

In 1887, the Early Closing Association, as part of the Victorian belief that a healthy body promotes a healthy mind, formed a Gymnasium Club that met in Old street. The benefits of such a club were extolled in the local newspaper.

'To those who will aid in making gymnastics more popular the reward will speedily come in seeing fewer bent backs coming from offices and shops, hearing fewer coughs from chests narrowed by stooping over their daily work, and knowing that increased numbers are recruiting their energies after the day's toil by a couple of hours hearty gymnastics instead of a couple of hours drinking from place to place.'[42]

The club's first two secretaries were an ironmonger's assistant, and a son who worked in the family's timber merchant business. By 1890 the club had 112 members, mainly shop workers and tradesmen, though now also attracting clerks, and was putting on displays of their skills in the Town Hall, attended by 'many of the leading families of the town.' Skills using swords, dumb bells, Indian clubs, and horizontal and parallel bars were on show as well as the art of boxing.[43] The gymnasium in Old Street was described in 1892.

'The clubroom has been thoroughly renovated and a new wood floor and windows put in. We also noted complete new sets of

The YHA building at 112, Corve Street that opened in 1932 welcomed up to 40 walkers and cyclists to Ludlow each day. For a small payment they were provided with a bed and had the use of a communal kitchen and common room.

(Courtesy of Shropshire Museum Service)

swords and foils ranged in racks on the walls – sufficient for all requirements. Hanging from the beams are two trapezes, a dozen rings etc. On the floor are the usual appliances of parallel and horizontal bars.'

In addition, the gymnasium had a floor span of 60ft by 20ft for drills and exercises and a new vaulting horse was on order. The instructor was a Mr Jagger late of the 15th Hussars.[44]

The Ludlow gymnasium had difficulties in keeping open during the 1890s and ultimately had to close down. One of the reasons given was that of class antagonism. This was not between classes but within a class as young middle-class men saw their social positions differently and refused to mix. As one correspondent explained:

'The 'young gentlemen' feels that his dignity would be endangered if he took part in any class with the young workmen. The embryo professional man shudders at the bare notion of standing in a line with a tradesman. The aristocratic and gentle soul of the bank clerk would be sullied if the owner rubbed shoulders with the lawyer's clerk.'[45]

A craze for roller-skating swept the country between 1908-1912 and the younger members of the town's middle and especially lower middle classes, enthusiastically joined in though admittedly two years after the craze began. The landlord of the *Golden Lion Hotel* asked the council in 1910 to allow him to use the top floor of the Town Hall as a skating venue. This request was turned down due to the fear of possible damage to the floor that was often used for dancing. Not to be thwarted, a Roller Skating Club hired the lower section of the Town Hall each Tuesday and Friday between 2pm and 11pm, even though skaters had to carefully avoid the pillars. Complaints soon flooded in from local residents due to the music, accompanying the skating, emanating through the open windows and keeping them awake.[46] A solution was found when the old British School at the top of Lower Broad Street

A roller skating craze hit Ludlow in 1910 and the main venue was soon the old British School at the top of Lower Broad Street. As well as the usual skating days special fancy dress events, complete with prizes, were held such as this one. Capped staff, such as the man on the far right, had their own smart braided uniforms.
(Author's collection)

opened as a rink. For the admission price of sixpence, that included the hire of skates, people could enjoy themselves every evening from 7pm to 10pm. Lessons, given by an instructor, could be had for one shilling per hour for 'plain skating' and 1/6d per hour for 'fancy skating.' In addition, a number of Fancy Dress Carnivals were held and the hall decorated. A clue as to the usual clientele attending can be discerned from the two initial winners. A tailor won the Gentleman's first prize and the winner for the Ladies competition was the wife of a printer.[47]

Though the craze soon wore off nationally it still thrived locally. As the *Ludlow Advertiser* pointed out 'in other places there are other amusements, while Ludlow is practically devoid of anything of the kind.'[48] Skating in Lower Broad Street carried on in the interwar years, though limited to Monday and Wednesday evenings. Social boundaries were now also crossed.

The Skating Rink employed its own instructor, Robert Thomas Rouse, photographed here in 1911, who gave lessons both for plain and 'fancy' skating both to newcomers and the more skilled. During the day he worked as a tailor.

(Courtesy of Shropshire Museum Service)

As no financial outlay was required in order to participate, other than the low entrance fee, more of the working classes found that they could now afford to skate. The Winter Garden, a new dance venue that opened in the Bull Ring in 1928, also offered occasional roller-skating from 1931.[49]

Away from the exuberance and physicality of youth, the middle classes of Ludlow found enjoyment in the sciences setting up a Natural History Society that collected new exhibits such as fossils for the local museum. As for the arts they were not only patrons attending the theatre and concerts, but participants in amateur dramatics and choirs. The first theatre in Ludlow was the Theatre Royal that was to be found towards the bottom of Mill Street opposite the boys grammar school and was opened in the late eighteenth century.[50] It held a maximum audience of three hundred people and had a pit, gallery and boxes. The theatre fell on hard times and closed for a time after the Assembly Rooms opened in 1840 and offered more modern and spacious surroundings.

A Mr Clifford, who already owned theatres in Shrewsbury, Worcester and Coventry, purchased the Mill Street premises and re-opened it as a theatre in 1856 and lit it by gas. Though in 1868 Christy's Minstrels were still performing 'to a large and fashionable audience,' and in 1875 it was being noted that 'some very excellent dramas and comedies are produced in a style which would reflect credit on a theatre of much larger pretensions than our local temple of Thespis,' this was becoming an increasing rarity. For a number of years the entertainment being offered was beginning to cater for a working-class audience as will be seen in the next chapter.[51]

Meanwhile, theatrical performances and concerts for the upper and middle classes were now being put on at the

The collection of geological specimens was a favourite pastime for some of the town's middle classes and the rich local fossil beds often meant that they hosted visits from other clubs and societies.
(Courtesy of Shropshire Museum Service)

Assembly Rooms on Castle Square. Ludlow's social hierarchy, and those attempting to climb the ladder to join them, attended what they considered more respectable, educational and morally uplifting performances.

As well as plays on tour following success in London, fashionable audiences attended evenings of Shakespeare, recitations from Dickens, opera and classical concerts. Whereas it was the Theatre Royal that suffered financially when the Assembly Rooms opened, it was the turn of the latter to face competition when the new Town Hall was built following the demolition of the Market Hall in 1887. Its newly constructed ballroom that could also be used as a theatre, now offered plays and concerts in more modern surroundings. The result was that the Assembly Rooms was offered for sale to the council in 1891 and then again in 1912. As will be seen in the following chapter, the rise of the cinema came to its rescue.

It was not always highbrow entertainment that was on offer at the Assembly Rooms and the new town hall; light

The local gentry still enjoyed their annual balls though a few by the interwar years had now moved away from the Assembly Rooms. Here in 1927 the Hunt ball was being held at Moor Park where the local 'bright young things' enjoyed themselves.

(Shropshire Museum Services)

entertainment had its place, especially after the closure of the Theatre Royal. Variety shows were sometimes offered where hypnotists, magicians, ventriloquists, comedians and singers could all be enjoyed. At Christmas, pantomimes were always popular, though the ticket prices that ranged from 6d to 3/-, with the cheaper tickets limited in number and no half price for children, showed that it was the middle classes who mainly enjoyed them.[52]

Lavish balls were also part of the social scene before the First World War. Many were annual events that included among others, the Agricultural Ball, the Ludlow Hunt Ball, the Ludlow Races Ball, and the Golf Club and Hockey Club Balls. Each is evidence of the social standing of their membership. The balls, where supper was also included, tended to start at 9pm and then the men in their evening dress and the ladies in their fine gowns danced the night away until the early hours of the morning, usually 3am but sometimes 5am. At the 1894 Agricultural Ball held at the town hall, the menu for the main course offered mayonnaise of salmon, dressed lobster, turkey a la royale, roulade of veal, galantine of turkey, ox tongues, chicken a la béchamel, pigeon pies, roast beef, veal and ham pies, York ham, raised game pies, and roast pheasant. The deserts that followed offered the choice of trifles, tipsy cakes, fruit and wine jellies, Italian creams, charlotte rouse, blancmange, patisserie francaise, mince pies, and maids of honour. Meanwhile in the same week, the same building housed a soup kitchen that helped alleviate the hunger of the town's poor and unemployed who queued in the winter cold.[53]

As well as enjoying the theatre productions and concerts as members of the audience, Ludlow's middle classes also participated. The Ludlow Choral Society was established in 1858 and held their early meetings at the music room in Raven Lane. By 1914 they had moved to Brand Lane. Their social credentials can be seen in that by 1890 their president was Lord Windsor and his four vice presidents were Sir C. H.

Rouse Boughton, the Honourable G. H. W. Windsor Clive, the Reverend R. Clayton, rector of St Laurence and Mayor John Valentine. The concerts included various musical and instrumental selections with visiting singers accompanied by local members who comprised the chorus.[54]

In 1900 the Ludlow Male Voice Choir was formed as an offshoot of the Choral Society. Forty members practised at the Ludford Parish Room and, as well as singing annually for the inmates of the workhouse, they gave regular concerts at the Town Hall. Both the choir and the choral society were still going strong during the interwar years and were joined by the Ludlow Amateur Glee Club in 1928. In addition, Ludlow had an Orchestral Society that was founded in 1901 that practised in the Congregational School Room.[55]

The middle classes also liked to tread the boards and the Ludlow Amateur Dramatic Society was formed in 1864. The social standing of its membership was shown when they put on a performance of Sheridan's *The Rivals* in 1869 in that they were supported by the instrumental section of the Ludlow Choral Society and could afford to hire their costumes from London.

At some point the society closed down, but it was resurrected in 1893 as the Ludlow Amateur Dramatic and Comedy Society only to be transformed yet again in 1907 back to the Ludlow Amateur Dramatic Society. At this date the secretary was an Arthur Bissell who owned a glass, china and earthenware wholesale and retail business in the High Street. This full turn of the circle did not end here and following the Great War it began life again as the Ludlow Dramatic and Operatic Society, rehearsals now taking place in the Music Room on Raven Lane. Throughout the interwar years the Society specialized in staging annual Gilbert and Sullivan operettas in addition to plays.[56]

They were not the only amateur performers in the town. In the last quarter of the nineteenth century the Ludlow Amateur Minstrels trod the Town Hall boards. Their 1894

For many the Ludlow Choral Society was an important part of middle class leisure time whether as participant or as part of the appreciative audience. Here the members celebrate their fiftieth anniversary with a grand concert at the Town Hall to a packed chamber. (Courtesy of Shropshire Museum Service)

performance was typical of their repertoire. What was then termed as a Negro Farce entitled 'Ebeneezer visited New York,' followed various banjo tunes, dialogues and comic duets. The popularity of amateur dramatics received another boost in 1930 with the formation of yet another group: the East Hamlet Amateur Dramatic Society which rehearsed in St Stephen's Hall and also put on annual performances at the Town Hall.[57]

Prior to 1914 upper and middle-class prejudice against those who were involved in trade, even though they might be wealthy or politically powerful in the town, permeated a number of sports and leisure pursuits. After the war, this began to dissipate though the middle classes as a whole still found it difficult to play or perform alongside members of the working classes. They were, however, happy to encourage them to pursue sports and recreational activities that they deemed 'respectable' or 'self improving,' though they preferred their own games, sports and leisure pursuits protected by club or society barriers. Most leisure activities by the mid twentieth century were still very much class riven.

Music made up an important part of middle class leisure time. The Ludlow Male Voice Choir, formed in 1900, was an offshoot of the Choral Society and they gave many concerts in places ranging from the Town Hall to the Workhouse. Here they are photographed in 1921. (Courtesy of Shropshire Museum Service)

CHAPTER 5

The Rise of Mass Entertainment

It has been seen how public houses had been, for many years, the focal point for working class-leisure, though they were coming under constant attack by many of the town's elite. With the encouragement of that same elite, sports and pastimes such as football and pigeon racing had also now become part of working class-culture. But other forces were at work. As living standards increased and working hours decreased, new areas of mass entertainment grew as the population at large embraced the rise of the cinema and the dance hall.

Even in the nineteenth century the working classes could join in and enjoy activities that were free. Whilst the middle classes could afford to attend concerts held in the Assembly Rooms and the town hall, the bulk of Ludlow's population were able to enjoy the promenade concerts that took place throughout the town during the summer months. They appear to have started in 1890 when the Early Closing Association organised a series of them on the Castle Green. By the following year the Ludlow Town Band were putting on free concerts on Whitcliffe. In 1901 the military Volunteer Band held a concert on the Castle Walk before being refused permission by Lord Powis. As a result the recitals truly became promenade concerts, moving to different localities around the town including Castle Square, the Bull Ring and Broad Street. These musical recitals began at 7pm and lasted two hours, usually on a Thursday.[1]

Such free concerts for the people carried on in the interwar years. In 1924 Ludlow Town Band could be found playing on the Castle Walk for 1½ hours on a Sunday evening, then on Castle Square on a Tuesday evening and the Bull Ring on a Thursday evening. The following year they had moved back to Whitcliffe where they performed on a Sunday afternoon. Grand Promenade Concerts, with visiting bands, were held on the Castle Green when admission was an affordable 6d.[2]

Ludlow Town Band, photographed here c1930, offered promenade concerts for the populace to enjoy from the 1890s and throughout the interwar years. During the summer months they played at various points around the town as well as on the castle walks and Whitcliffe.
(Courtesy of Jenny Finister Yapp Angell)

Travelling entertainers also provided free amusement. John Rounds, a frequent visitor to Ludlow market, sang ballads, whilst street organs often entertained the passing crowds. One inebriated gentleman in 1906 found himself before the magistrates' bench for dancing to the music.[3] Arthur Everall recalled street entertainment at the Buttercross in the 1890s.

> *'On market days there was a scene of animation. As well as the market stands, the portly farm wives brought their butter, eggs and poultry for sale and sat near the kerb with their wares. Much free entertainment was available in the shape of one-man bands, dancing bears, Punch and Judy shows, a gentleman without arms who wrote copperplate with his toes and, of course, some gypsies and Welsh harpists.'*[4]

Fishing was also a free leisure pursuit. Admittedly, stretches of the River Teme required permission to fish or the need to join the elite local Angling Club that was allowed a limited number of rods on the waters above Dinham weir. However, free fishing could be enjoyed in the public waters on the Whitcliffe side of the River Teme between Dinham and Mill Street weirs.

Swimming and nudity

Swimming could also be enjoyed and the River Corve, and especially the River Teme, became a playground for the people of Ludlow. The river had always been the place where Ludlow's youth had learnt to swim, especially in the waters just above the Mill Street Weir. At first this was left to individuals but in 1910 the Grammar School, the Commercial School at the top of Mill Street, and the National Schools were allowed to use the two bathing huts on the riverbank. This in turn meant that each school could give swimming lessons in the river.

Soon the Girls High School and the Church Lads Brigade joined them. For many local schoolchildren, their schools were still using the river to teach swimming in the 1940s.[5]

But not even bathing was immune to falling foul of middle-class disapproval. Before 1914 many working-class families could not afford to buy swimming costumes for their children with the result that nude bathing or bathing in underwear was quite usual. This, alongside the excited chatter, often interspersed with colourful language, upset many middle-class people, especially ladies, as they promenaded on the Bread Walk and Whitcliffe. That this often happened on

Fishing was a pastime enjoyed by all classes and all ages on stretches of the River Teme that did not require a permit.
(Courtesy of Shropshire Museum Service)

The river was the town's swimming pool, especially the section at the bottom of Mill Street where local schools offered their pupils swimming lessons. These boys are from the Grammar School and could afford costumes whilst many local children swam either in their underwear or in the nude, much to the shocked annoyance of middle class walkers enjoying the Bread Walk.
(Courtesy of Shropshire Museum Service)

a Sunday just added to the affront they felt. The result was constant complaints and requests for police and council action.

In 1894, nude or semi-nude bathing was so prevalent that the police arrested four teenagers from Lower Galdeford for not wearing proper bathing dress whilst swimming in the river. The police told the court that they had brought this case as a warning to others. In 1898, eleven young men from the Galdeford area and Raven Lane were arrested for nude bathing at the bottom of Lower Mill Street at 4pm on a Sunday afternoon in what appears was a planned operation following numerous complaints. In addition, it was claimed that they were cavorting both on the weir and the riverbank using obscene language. As a result, 'several respectable people on the Whitcliffe, walking along the lower walk … turned back, especially the ladies.' Punishment was far from light. Eight of the defendants were fined between 5/- and 10/6d or, if not paid, between five to fourteen days imprisonment.[6]

The problem persisted and the mayor, as magistrate, asked the police in 1905 to try to stop men swimming naked in the Teme and then climbing out onto the Whitcliffe bank in full view of those taking a stroll. At a council meeting the same year the matter became a heated topic of discussion. One councillor pointed out that 'ladies in the town had to shun the Whitcliffe owing to the indecent acts of a few hooligans' who lay around in, what he claimed, was 'a naked state.' It appears he was objecting to men sunbathing in their swimwear and wanted the police to ask them to move nearer the riverbank.

Another councillor pointed out that 'at present an undesirable state of things occurred owing to men dressing and undressing.' He asked if it would be possible to erect a canvas screen behind which men could change. The influence of the church was felt when it was also requested that a by-law be passed to stop bathing in the river after 10am on a Sunday morning when religious services began. The Town Clerk had to remind the council that this had already been attempted and the Home Office had refused to sanction such a law.[7]

The problem of nudity and semi nudity abated in the interwar years though the use of the local rivers as a popular leisure facility did not. As was pointed out when the possibility of the construction of a local swimming baths was discussed:

> *'In the (river) were a number of youngsters, boys and girls, enjoying bathing and swimming. Previously in the evening I had met a number of young ladies processing down Corve Street, carrying bathing costumes and towels, on their way ostensibly to some secluded spot in the river to bathe.'* [8]

Calls for a public swimming pool, however, though often made, were constantly sidelined due to fears of cost and how this would impact on the ratepayers of the town. The attempt in 1938 to have one built by the council was a close run thing with supporters losing by only one vote.[9]

The fact that one bank of the River Teme at Ludlow was taken up by the common land of Whitcliffe meant that events that took place on the river could also be enjoyed for nothing. The annual swimming races held by the Bathing Club (later Swimming Club) began in 1867 and were still being held until the outbreak of the Second World War. All these could be watched from the far bank for free. These included special events such as traversing the greasy pole, rowing races whilst sitting astride barrels, and water polo matches.

The regattas

For a number of years before the Great War, all the people of Ludlow could use the Whitcliffe bank to watch the spectacles

The finish line in 1905 and 1908-1910 was at Dinham Bridge and here the crowd, with the ladies dressed in their finery and many of the men sporting boaters, are waiting to cheer on the crews as they come to the final yards of the race. (Courtesy of Shropshire Museum)

The starting line for the regatta races held on the lower stretches of the river was just above the Mill Street weir. Here crowds assembled on the Bread Walk opposite to enjoy the excitement.
(Courtesy of Shropshire Museum Service)

of annual regattas that were the brainchild of Alderman Lloyd the chairman of the town's Attractions Committee. The result was that a middle-class leisure pursuit became a popular working-class entertainment.

The genesis of these regattas was the purchase by the committee in 1905 of three boats, using monies borrowed from the Town Council. They were named in a christening ceremony: Whitcliffe, Ludlow Castle and Harry Lloyd. They were two double sculled boats and one single sculled to be used for pleasure on the river by visitors to the town. At first they were boarded from a platform at the Mill Street Weir, before the landing platform moved to the opposite bank just below Dinham Bridge. Boats could be hired from 1pm each day until dark, and rowers and their passengers were charged 6d for one hour.[10]

A year later permission was obtained to use the waters above Dinham Weir to Batty island and, as a result, five more boats were purchased including Alice, Arts and Crafts, King Edward VII, and Comus. Six now plied their trade on the upper waters and two below Dinham Bridge. Demand often exceeded supply and this resulted in two more boats being bought in 1913. So successful was the whole venture that not only visitors enjoyed a time on the river but also the townsfolk. The boats were still for hire throughout the interwar years when they totalled eleven, four more being obtained some to replace older craft.[11] Boating was still popular during the war years. In 1941 the council took over the responsibility for the twelve boats and the boathouse from the Attractions Committee and continued to run them. Kate Deeley recalls being on the river in them during time off for her school certificate examinations. Her companions were boys from Lancing College who had been evacuated here and also RAF servicemen billeted in Ludford Park.[12]

As an added entertainment for the watching crowd novelty races and events were held. Traversing a greasy pole stretched over the water was one and another, photographed here, was a barrel race.
(Courtesy of Shropshire MuseumService)

The first regatta, in 1905, was based around the first purchased boats. It was held on the stretch of river between Mill Street weir and Dinham Bridge, a course of 400 yards rowing upstream. There were four competitions: sculls and double sculls both for men and women. Several hundred spectators watched from both banks, but those on the Whitcliffe side did not have to pay and that reduced income. As a result the following two regattas took place on the waters above Dinham weir. In 1906 the Swimming club joined the day's entertainment with its own annual sports. In addition, popular

The middle classes could afford to pay the entry fee for the bank opposite the Whitcliffe. Here they could sit on seats rather than stand on the steep slopes or sit on the grass on the free side. They could also enjoy the comfort of taking tea in the shelter of a marquee or enjoy the music of the town band.

(Courtesy of Shropshire Museum Service)

The Whitcliffe was the playground for the people of Ludlow especially the children who could spend hours on their own there. In the summer games of all kinds could be played whilst in the winter snowball fights and tobogganing would be enjoyed.
(Courtesy of Shropshire Museum Service)

events such as traversing the greasy pole and barrel races were introduced. About 700 paying spectators, congregated on the eastern bank, looked on, but the bend in the river meant that only 250 yards of the course could be seen. To counter this, in 1907 the spectators moved over to Swans Nest Meadow on the opposite bank where the entire course could be seen, but this meant that paying spectators had to enter via Oakley Park with the result that attendance was only deemed 'satisfactory.'[13]

The organisers now bowed to the inevitable and the regatta moved back to its original position with the result that the crowds grew considerably in size with some travelling by train from the Midland cities. But the problem of being unable to charge spectators who chose to watch from Whitcliffe bank remained. An attempt to collect donations, by having volunteers go amongst the crowd with collecting boxes, had limited success. This, added to poor weather, caused the regattas to accrue losses and 1910 saw the final one. This popular and free entertainment for the masses had come to an end though the annual swimming sports carried on.[14] The Whitcliffe still remained, however, as a playground for the people of the town as an editorial in the local newspaper pointed out just a few weeks before the Great War broke out.

Before the advent of the cinema and the dance hall, one way of meeting the opposite sex was to stroll along the Bread Walk on a Sunday dressed to impress. It was also the place for young mothers to enjoy the fresh air with their babies.
(Courtesy of Shropshire Museum Service)

Some parades were very formal such as this one walking down Old Street in 1897 headed by the police followed by the mayor, aldermen and councillors. The size of such processions can be discerned by the fact that its end appears to stretch past the Bull Ring. (Courtesy of Shropshire Museum Service)

> *'It was a quite a common sight to see parties laden with lunch baskets proceeding in the direction of Whitcliffe and the woods. The ladies turned out in summer frocks (and) many straw boaters worn.'*[15]

Until the passing of the Holidays with Pay Act 1938 gave some workers the legal right to one week's paid annual holiday per year, all holidays taken were without pay. As a result for most working-class adults, holidays away from Ludlow, or even just days out, were rare. It is easy to forget just how insular life was for so many in the town. Workers outings, paid for by their employers were, therefore, a special

Other parades, such as this one in Broad Street, were more of a spectacle with gaily-clad horsemen and organisations such as the Oddfellows carrying brightly coloured banners.
(Courtesy of Shropshire Museum Service)

treat. These began at the beginning of the twentieth century. In 1899, thirty employees of Gaius Smith, grocers, along with a few guests, were taken to Church Stretton to ramble over the hills, with tea provided at a local hotel. The building firm of Turford and Southward took their workers to Blackpool for the day. Arriving at the seaside at 6.20 in the morning employees enjoyed a full day on the promenade and beach with lunch provided at the Central Station Restaurant, before setting off for home on the 9pm train. Messrs J Roberts of the Phoenix works also took their workers to Blackpool, treating them to lunch at the Promenade Restaurant. In 1911 Marstons, the corn merchants, paid for their 46 employees to see a pageant in London. Such outings continued into the interwar years, with the staff of Ludlow's Steam Laundry on Corve Street having a day out in Weston-Super-Mare.[16]

Ludlow Agricultural Show

During this period of unpaid holidays, local parades, fêtes and galas were always looked forward to with anticipation and enjoyed to the full. Being free or with a low entrance charge, attendance was often numbered in thousands. As expected in a country town, the largest and longest-running event was the annual Ludlow Agricultural Show that was first held in 1847 on the Castle Green. It continued to be held there until it moved to Ludford Park in 1894 as it 'had grown too big for the (place) in which it is held.' Now it could comfortably house crowds numbering in the thousands.[17]

As the years passed, the show at first underwent only slow change. In 1875 the organisers were congratulating themselves on keeping up old traditions, proudly declaring:

> *'This is one of the few societies which adheres to the old custom of awarding prizes to labourers and servants for excellence in their calling, frugality, honesty, abstinence and long servitude.'*

A prize was even awarded 'to the man who by his daily labour, has reared the greatest number of children without parochial aid, having a good character.' In that year a James Prosser, employed on the Oakley Hall Estate since 1837, and who had brought up ten children, the youngest of which was now eleven years old, was the proud winner.[18] This form of *noblesse oblige* still could be found in 1904 when a prize was awarded to the farm labourer who had worked for the same employer for the greatest length of time. Similar awards were given to the longest-serving farm female servant and to the longest-serving male and female Ludlow domestic servants.[19]

As the nineteenth century ended, change speeded up. In 1898 a military tournament was held alongside the usual agricultural competitions and demonstrations, attracting a record attendance. The special attraction in 1911 was the launch of a hot air balloon that landed at Clee Stanton with the two men on board being brought back by car to a large

A number of parades, especially the ones where collections were held to help various charities, were designed for crowd enjoyment and often ended in prizes being awarded for the best fancy dress or decorated cart, cycle or even pram. This photograph shows three such participants in the yard behind the Portcullis public house on Upper Galdeford preparing to for their public appearance. (Courtesy of Shropshire Museum Service)

ovation. For the first time a number of variety artistes were hired to entertain the crowd in 1923. These included acrobats, clowns and tightrope walkers. By 1927, as well as the usual judging of the best farm animals in their numerous categories, there was also one for 'the best specimens of typical British Girls.' That same year the whole event was filmed and shown at the local Picture House.[20]

The year 1878 saw Ludlow dress up for a special occasion when the town was chosen to host the Shropshire and

West Midlands Agricultural Show. Though held in Ludford Park, the town's welcome started at the railway station since many visitors came by train. At the junction of Station Road and Corve Street 'the bunting came into view. A pretty arch was seen near the turn with the motto 'We give you a hearty welcome' and on the reverse 'We hope you will visit us again.' The main streets and major buildings were festooned in flags and painted canvasses. Decorated arches spanned most roads, many decorated with evergreens, and others with further mottos. The arch at the Buttercross read 'Labour conquers all things' whilst the one where Galdeford meets Tower Street read 'Welcome to our ancient borough.' The correspondent from the *Hereford Times* was very impressed saying that 'Ludlow presented a pleasing and novel appearance, the bright colours

Much time and effort went into the preparations for carnival parades. At this 1920's event, proud mothers surround these six young girls in their matching dresses who are ready to pull a decorated pram acting as a coach, complete with two young boys dressed as attendants. (Courtesy of Claire Powick Hainsworth)

of the flags, mixed up with the dark buildings, reminded one of some of the old Spanish towns with its gay awnings.'[21]

Parades, processions and fêtes

Processions through the town, organised by various community groups, comprised of marching bands, decorated vehicles of all kinds, and manned by people in fancy dress, became a popular entertainment. Those taking part, and the crowds that lined the streets to cheer them, enjoyed such events. All were a noisy, colourful, and a welcome distraction from the rather drab lives lived by many. Fêtes and Galas put on by the Foresters and Oddfellows Lodges, held every four to five years, attracted crowds in the thousands, many often coming from miles

1923 saw the first May Queen pageant. After a procession through the town's streets, the young woman was crowned amidst much pomp and ceremony on the Castle Green.

(Courtesy of Shropshire Museum Service)

away. As early as 1863, special trains brought in 300 Foresters Lodge members and their families from Shrewsbury and 700 from South Wales to join local members and the townsfolk in general. That year the crowds enjoyed games and amusements on the Castle Green, followed by dancing in the evening.[22]

At the 1890 Foresters fête and gala, which attracted nearly 5,000 people, the day started with a procession through the town to Ludford Park that was led by the local lodge's banner and the Shropshire Artillery Band. They were followed by characters from the tale of Robin Hood, members in full regalia on horseback, members walking two abreast, a wagon decorated by trees representing the widows and orphans section, the juvenile members, the Ludlow Rifle Volunteers Band, Ludlow Fire Brigade with their horse-pulled engine, and, finally, members of other local Lodges carrying their District banners. In the afternoon, in addition to the usual side shows and stalls, a six-a-side football match was held followed by horse and pony races and athletic events, all alongside entertainment from a tightrope walker and a magic show by a Professor Le Roche, Man of Mystery. As was usual the day ended with dancing.[23] The Oddfellows fête of 1894 included a military tournament to entertain the 3,000 spectators that flocked to Ludford Park. Once again the day started with a large procession through the town that included three bands. As well as the usual stalls and sports the military gave demonstrations of tent pegging, bayonet exercises and drill.[24]

From 1905, the people of Ludlow enjoyed an annual Charity Parade. As we saw in the previous chapter, the Cycle Club held a fancy dress parade each year to raise funds for the medical care of the townsfolk. This ended in 1902 but was revived as a general working-man's parade raising money for the same cause. The parades were now held on a Saturday rather than a Thursday so that more people could enjoy the day's fun. The first of the new parades started at the *Portcullis Inn* and made its way up Galdeford, went along Gravel Hill

The crowning of carnival queens remained a mainstay of public pageants after the Second World War as this 1947 photograph shows. Such events now attracted the formal participation of the town's civic dignitaries. (Shropshire Museum Services)

to the *Raven Inn* at the junction with New Road, before turning back to retrace its steps. It then made its way to Castle Square via Tower Street, King Street and the High Street. It was here that the judging took place for the best fancy dress costumes, both adult and child, the best decorated cycle and the best decorated car, cart or dray. Throughout the procession a charitable collection was made from the crowds lining the streets. Each year up to 1914 the parade underwent change to add fresh enjoyment for the crowds. Decorated prams joined in, decorated motor cars replaced bicycles, whilst further bands played, and maypole dancing by local schoolchildren could be enjoyed in the square. On such days the townsfolk came out to play.[25]

In the interwar years such events continued to be extremely popular and tended to follow the same pattern of earlier years. In 1923, the Young Men's Christian Association (YMCA) organised the first May Queen Pageant on the

Castle Green. The entertainment included Morris, Maypole and Folk dancing and a parade of schoolchildren dressed in various costumes. All was followed by a dance in the evening with free entry. The following year saw fancy and comic dress competitions as well as prizes for the best decorated cars, drays, cycles, prams and even handcarts. The day began with a grand parade from East Hamlet to the castle led by a band. Two queens were in attendance: last year's May Queen and the present year's Rose Queen. They were served by courtiers and court ladies dressed in historical costumes inspired by the middle ages, and trumpeters heralded the crowning. In addition, local schoolchildren entertained the crowd with dances.[26]

Air displays

Air displays also enthralled the populace at large, As early as 1913, one was organised by the town's attractions committee in Ludford park that was watched by a crowd of over 4,000. Though these paid an entrance fee, many hundreds more watched free of charge from viewing points such as Steventon. The aviator, Bentfield Charles Hucks, the first pilot to perform a loop, flew a 70 hp Bleriot monoplane and the highlight was when he dropped a number of exploding bombs and finally a parachutist. No one, however, took up his offer of becoming a passenger at £5 a ride. It was different just after the war when people queued to experience a flight in a three-seater Avro that took off from the racecourse. The charge was from one guinea upwards depending on the distance and time travelled, so most of the town could not afford such a treat, but all could watch for free. In 1924, the Berkshire Aviation Company came to Ludlow to offer further leisure trips in two aircraft: a three seater and a five seater. Over one hundred people took a flight over Ludlow watched in awe by the rest of the town. In 1933 'one of the largest Civil Air Pageants ever held in the country' took place at Winders Farm in aid of Ludlow Cottage Hospital. Fifteen aircraft took part and three of the pilots were women.

Once again passenger flights were offered to those who could afford them whilst thousands watched the derring-do of the aviators as they performed their acrobatic air displays.[27]

From 1929 the Ludlow Trades Association organised an annual Civic and Shopping Week. This event began with a carnival procession, once again headed by a band, and included an array of brightly-dressed vehicles, both motorised and horse-drawn. As well as a fancy dress competition, the 1930 event included beauty competitions whilst in 1933 two visiting film stars, Daphne Courtney and Jimmy Godden, took pride of place.[28] From 1931, the British Legion organised a combined athletic sports, fête, and horse show every August Bank Holiday, initially in Ludford Park and then in Oakley Park. The event was preceded in 1933 by a parade through

In 1913, Bentfield Charles Hucks brought his Bleriot monoplane to Ludford Park. Over 4,000 paying spectators watched as he performed various aerial acrobatics though no one dared take up his offer of flying with him. (Courtesy of Shropshire Museum Service)

In the interwar years flying displays were more frequently seen over Ludlow and in 1933, in aid of the local Cottage Hospital, an air pageant with fifteen aircraft was held. As well as flying displays, many people took advantage of paying for a flight over the town.
(Courtesy of Shropshire Museum Service)

the town starting at Station Drive whilst by 1936, after it had moved to the grounds of Henley Hall, over 5,000 spectators took part in the day's events.[29]

Masque of Comus

By far the largest public event of the interwar years took place in July 1934. To celebrate the tercentenary of the first staging of Milton's *Masque of Comus* a re-enactment took place in the Castle, preceded by an historical pageant The staging of the play was to be preceded by an historical pageant with a cast of 3,000 in full costume, a chorus of 200 and an orchestra of 100. This pageant was in five episodes starting with the story of Wild Edric and his bride Godda, whilst other episodes included the bones of St Milburga being taken to Wenlock Priory and the departure of the young Edward V and his brother from Ludlow Castle never to be seen again. The pageant was held over six days and in addition to the daily performances, there

As well as showing a production of Milton's Masque of Comus, the 1934 pageant showed five historical episodes from history enacted all in full costume. (Courtesy of Shropshire Museum Service)

were also three evening showings. The audience was housed in a covered auditorium that could hold 4,000.[30]

Theatre and cinema

Entertainment for the working classes that required payment that they could afford slowly grew over the years. The Theatre Royal at the bottom of Mill Street had catered for an upper and middle-class audience but with the opening of the Assembly Rooms in 1840 they slowly had been transferring their custom. To keep in business the theatre began to adapt its repertoire for a new audience. By 1869 cheap concerts for the people were being offered: 4d for the boxes, 3d for the pit and 2d for the gallery. Comic songs and musical acts now attracted crowds that queued prior to the doors opening and for some performances scores had to be turned away. The theatre was now evolving into Ludlow's Music Hall. Evidence of the changing social makeup of those attending can be seen when a local amateur company put on a performance. The audience was described as working class and it was noted the 'the gallery portion, … generally rather noisy, maintained excellent order from first to last,' presumably because normally they were far rowdier. Once, when a Miss Tusk, a young lady who had recently come to live in Ludlow, sang the song *Up in a Balloon*, she was met with 'deafening shouts of applause' especially from those in the cheaper gallery seats. At yet another concert, when comic and sing-along songs were prevalent, the finale was a 'comical side-splitting negro burlesque entitled *The Darky Soldier*.' During this performance, when a pony was brought on to the stage and refused to move because it became frightened by the noise and the gaslights, it caused 'raucous enjoyment.' At another show one of the performers came on the stage drunk and started fighting with a fellow member of

In order to help boost local business as a world wide economic recession struck in 1929, the Ludlow Trades Organisation organised an annual Shopping Week that began with a carnival procession. As the messages on this entry appear to show, not all thought that the committee was doing enough.

(Courtesy of Shropshire Museum Service)

the cast, again to the great entertainment of the audience. The theatre finally closed in 1879.[31]

Theatre for the people now moved to a new venue. Up until the Great War various portable travelling theatres visited Ludlow catering for working class entertainment with prices to suit their pocket: just 3d for the gallery, 6d for the pit and one shilling for the front stalls. That one shilling for the most expensive seats would not purchase any ticket for a performance at the Assembly Rooms or the Town Hall. The Smithfield, off Lower Galdeford, was the usual place for such theatres to be erected, with a troupe being given a performing licence for up to three months at a time. Such shows, offering variety acts, interspersed with short comedies or farces, drew 'large audiences nightly' and a claim that 'anyone who wanted a hearty laugh should pay a visit.' The noisy participation of the audience was shown when, during a comedy play, the

1934 saw the largest pageant that the town had ever seen with a costumed cast of 3,000 plus orchestra and chorus, all watched by an audience of 4,000 housed in a covered auditorium within the grounds of the castle.
(Author's collection)

amorous intentions of a character appeared too slow, the crowd gave vocal advice on how to speed the courtship up. At times, due to the popularity of shows, fights broke out both inside and outside the theatre. This could be due to argumens over seating caused by overcrowding, or through some audience members being unable to hear the performers because of the noisy interjections of neighbours.[32]

In the early twentieth century some of these travelling theatres, such as Sinclair's Palace, began to show one of the new cinemagraphic films as a finale to a full music hall programme. These were replaced by 1914 with travelling shows such as Manders and Sons Electric Cinema Theatre. Still situated on the Smithfield, such visitors put on two film performances a night to 'bumper crowds.' Their first programme began with scenes from the Delhi Durbar followed by other short films such as *The Pony Express* and *The Outlaw Samaritan*. Films changed each night and audiences could then watch, among others, *The Big Detective*, *Cattle Rustler's End*, *The Siege of Calais* and *The Funeral of Edward VII*. Thus began the age of the cinema in Ludlow.[33]

In 1912 Alfred Temple and his wife took over the Picture Hall in the Assembly Rooms where occasional films had been shown since 1909. For two nights, Mondays and Tuesdays at 8pm, the Temples put on a series of short films. The programme then changed for Wednesdays and Thursdays and then changed again for Fridays and Saturdays. As an example, one evening's wide offerings were *Canals and Rivers of Siam*, *Stolen Letter* (drama), With her Card (drama), *Lady Godiva* (historical), *1776* (war drama), *Inconstant Percy* (comedy) and *Stray Bullets* (comedy).[34]

The popularity of this new form of entertainment ensured that constant improvements were being made to ensure that not only full houses could be kept up but also that the number of shows on offer could be increased.[35] In 1912 Temple informed his customers that 'to keep the hall sweet and

Ludlow's original theatre on Mill Street, opposite the Boy's Grammar School, closed in 1879 and was developed as two residential properties with the same façade. Its place, offering a Music Hall type of entertainment for the working classes, was taken over by travelling theatres that set up for business on the Smithfield. (Courtesy of Shropshire Museum Services)

cool during the hot weather, sprays will be used; also a large electric ceiling fan is being installed as soon as possible.' Later that same year new tip-up seats, as found in good theatres, were installed in the front rows and new equipment purchased that was far quieter and gave a steadier picture. In 1913 a new operating room, lined with sheet iron as a fire precaution, was built outside the main auditorium and films projected through a hole in the wall. As well as being safer and quieter this also enabled further seating to be added.[36]

In the same year the whole Picture House was redecorated and modernised. Electric lighting was installed whilst the old gas chandeliers were kept but now just hid new ventilation ducts. The balcony was carpeted, two thirds of the seats were now of the new tip-up variety whilst the remaining ones were repainted and varnished. In addition, to accompany these silent films, a band was now hired to replace the pianoforte used previously. Between films, ex-music hall artistes were employed to keep audiences entertained whilst film reels were changed.[37]

In 1921 the Picture House underwent expansion with a new gallery built above the balcony. A staircase was constructed behind the ticket office that rose to the back of the new gallery and there was now a broad gangway down the centre of the seating. A café for patrons was also opened. In 1932, when the cinema was taken over by the Ludlow Picture House Company, further improvements were made. The cinema was closed for two weeks whilst an 'army of decorators from London' moved in. Seating was reduced from 560 to 500 to improve comfort and the whole cinema was carpeted throughout. A year later a new sound system was installed and the cinema was said to be the most up-to-date in all Shropshire.[38]

The length of film shown also underwent rapid change with the numerous short films being replaced with longer feature films. In October 1912 the film *The Three Musketeers* was shown that lasted half an hour whilst a year later when *Quo Vadis* was featured it ran for two hours. Just a few weeks later *Les Miserables* was viewed over a period of two hours plus. With the advent of full-length feature films, the timings of shows changed. There would be two shows per week: Monday to Wednesday and Thursday to Saturday. By 1921 there were two performances every evening at 5.15pm and 8.30pm with three performances on a Saturday, the extra one a matinee performance for children at 2.30pm. From 1932 there were other matinee performances for adults on Mondays and Thursdays and sometimes a midnight performance on a Friday. The coming of the 'talkies' to Ludlow on Whit Monday 1930, with the showing of *King of the Khyber Rifles*, also saw the appearance of the British Movietone News on the screen.[39]

For most of the interwar years the Picture House was the only cinema in Ludlow. For a short time, just after the

Great War, it faced competition from one using the Town Hall. In 1920 a Mr E. P. Norton was granted a licence to show films at the Town hall on Thursdays, Fridays and Saturdays at 6pm and 8pm. In September this was increased to six days a week. Though the 300 seats were filled on some nights, the business failed. It changed hands in March 1921 but finally closed at the end of that year.[40]

Serious competition came on the horizon when the council passed plans in August 1935 for the building of a second cinema, to be called the Clifton, on Old Street. This required the demolition of a number of properties and it was finally opened to the public on Saturday 24 September 1938 amidst great pomp and ceremony, including a guest appearance by Miss Jean Gillie a twenty-year-old starlet of the screen.

This new 'picture palace' had three sets of doors at its entrance that opened onto a spacious foyer where the ticket office was located. Decorative plasterwork was everywhere and a staircase, with portraits of film stars of the day, took you up to the balcony lounge that had scenic paintings covering its walls. Everywhere was carpeted and the tip-up seats were covered in terracotta velvet. 508 cinemagoers could be seated in the auditorium and a further 204 in the balcony. Orange-coloured curtains drew back to show silver ones that in turn revealed the cinema screen. This screen sat on a stage 12ft deep that the owners claimed could be used for community events such as amateur theatre. Uniformed staff were everywhere, from a commissionaire who controlled queues and welcomed customers, to an army of usherettes to guide you to your seats and 'that were at your service with chocolates, cigarettes and ices.'[41] For many in Ludlow, who often lived in damp, one-up one-down houses lit by gas lamps and candles, this must have seemed like a taste of their own Hollywood glamour, a step into a fantasy world for a few hours.

And it was the working classes who made up most of the cinema audience in its early decades. The main reason for this was that, as well as being glamorous, cinema admission was also cheap. The most expensive seats at the Picture House in 1912 were 1/-. This was cheaper than the cheapest seat at a concert or play at the Town Hall. Ticket prices remained low throughout the interwar years. When the 'talkies' arrived in Ludlow in 1930, it was possible to purchase a ticket for 6d, and 1/- would obtain for you a very good seat, and prices had not changed when the Clifton Cinema opened in 1938. What this meant was that an afternoon or night out at the 'pictures' was within reach of the purse strings of all including the unemployed. For this group, as well as being somewhere warm and comfortable, the cinema was a place to forget their everyday troubles for a few hours.

The Clifton Cinema, purpose built, opened in Old Street in 1938 giving the people of Ludlow the choice of two places to visit and, therefore, twice as many films to watch.

(Courtesy of Shropshire Museum Service)

Women made up an important part of the audience numbers, especially working-class mothers in the afternoon. A matinee performance could be watched between the daily shop and the return of the children from school. For many women who did not like to visit a public house, the cinema was the first real opportunity to enjoy a leisure pursuit. That cinema-going was seen as part of the culture of many working-class women by the 1940s can be seen in the contents of a letter sent to the Chief Billeting Officer of the Stanton Lacy area. A middle-class lady, who was trying her best to put forward reasons why she should not have such women sent to live with her, hints none too subtly, that their idea of a social life would not be her own or that of her class. 'Whatever we say here,' she points out 'they will all want to be nearer the town with shops and the cinema.'[42]

Young couples also made up a large section of the cinemagoers. As will be seen, young women tended to meet young men at the dance halls that blossomed in the first half of the twentieth century, but the cinema was where courtship often took place. The darkness allowed them the privacy to kiss and fondle, especially in the double seats at the back, away from the eyes of family and neighbours.

People visited the cinema twice or even three times a week. This was because, for many, it was not a specific film they went to see but to take part in a social occasion, to join in a communal atmosphere. In a way, going to watch a film was similar, at first, to attending the Music Hall with the enjoyment of audience participation. There would be catcalls and whistles, cheering for the cowboys and boos for the Indians or the rustlers being chased by the posse. Villains were hissed and heroes warned to look behind them. Technical faults also caused humorous outbursts. Musical chants such as 'Why are we waiting' would be heard or slow handclapping started. When the 'talkies' arrived, to try to change such behaviour, many cinemas put up notices asking their patrons to be quiet

The Clifton Cinema was a 'picture palace' offering townsfolk who often lived in small, cramped cottages, often only lit by gaslight, a night of pampered luxury. Lit by electricity, everywhere was carpeted and uniformed usherettes guided you to your velvet-covered seat and served you with chocolates, cigarettes and ice creams. (Courtesy of the Assembly Rooms)

during the showing of films so that the dialogue could be heard. In Ludlow this did not take place to the annoyance of some. It was pointed out that when anything amusing occurred the audience still tended to laugh for too long so that the next five or six lines could not be discerned.[43] Also, if the soundtrack failed to match the lips on screen, vocal jocular reminders to the management were made. By the 1950s audience interruptions still occurred, such as when, during a scene where suspense is being purposely built up and the audience was holding its breath, the loud bursting of a crisp packet could cause paroxysms of relieved laughter. Saturday shows for children could also be anarchic with constant chatter and seat swapping.

The wireless

Another form of mass entertainment that swept the nation in the interwar years was the coming of the radio or wireless as it was then known. An exhibition was held at the Brand Lane Hall in 1926 to publicise this new addition to the home, and in 1934 a special advertisement feature in the *Ludlow Advertiser* listed seven local shops specialising in selling them. Not only had they come down in price but also a wireless could be

The first full time cinema in Ludlow was set up in 1912 in a section of the Assembly Rooms and called itself the Picture House. Its popularity can be judged by the queues waiting to enter in this photograph from 1942. It was pressure from the armed forces that forced the local magistrates to allow films to be shown on a Sunday in Ludlow, the last town in Shropshire to do so.
(Courtesy of Shropshire Museum Service)

purchased on hire purchase terms that brought one into the reach of most families. By 1938 over nine million licences had been issued which meant that 98% of the population had access to this new form of entertainment.[44] In Ludlow, as many households still did not have access to electricity, their wireless was powered by an accumulator. This would last about a week before the batteries had to be recharged. The family of Eileen Reynolds took theirs to a garage on Gravel Hill.[45] Unlike most leisure activities of the time, the wireless was a family entertainment rather than for the individual. All could sit around the wireless of an evening and listen to drama, comedy and music.

The music heard at home helped in the development of another new form of mass entertainment: that of the dance halls. The BBC had its own house band in 1926: the London Radio Dance Band. By the 1930s several hours a week would be devoted to light dance music with popular bands such as that of Victor Sylvester being heard by avid listeners. It is difficult to exaggerate the importance of dancing at this time as a leisure activity. Alongside the public house and the cinema, it was a major influence on the lives of the working classes. For the first time it was possible to find a labourer in the arms of a bank clerk's daughter whilst they enjoyed a waltz. Social barriers on the dance floor were at their lowest. It was also where most couples met for the first time and the courting ritual began. It is no surprise that so many in Ludlow felt saddened when the old Town Hall was demolished in the 1980s, since that was where so many married couples first met.

Dance Halls and Social Balls

As was seen in Chapter 4, for most of the nineteenth century the upper and middle classes attended lavish balls, with the gentlemen dressed in formal white tie evening-wear and the ladies in ball gowns. By the turn of the century dances rather than balls began to be held both at the Assembly Rooms and

Even at this Young Conservatives Ball held at 22 Broad Street in the 1930s, dress codes were changing. Though bow ties and evening dress were still worn by some men others wore ties with a lounge suit. It was the same with the ladies: ball dresses for some, skirts for others. (Courtesy of Shropshire Museum Service)

the Town Hall. Those attending were from slightly lower down the social scale. The Ludlow Football Club started to hold annual dinner dances to raise funds, and in 1913 the Amalgamated Union of Shop Assistants organised a dance, complete with 'refreshments.' Rather than dance to an orchestra, a band would supply the music. As for dress, men could now wear a dinner or even a lounge suit whilst their partners could wear evening dresses. Dances were no longer confined to the Assembly Rooms and the Town Hall but now took place at the *Charlton Arms Hotel* where the stables were converted into a dance hall, the *George Hotel* in the Market Square, the music room in Raven Lane and at the skating rink at the top of Lower Broad Street.[46]

The number of venues increased further in the interwar years as dancing as a leisure activity for all took off. Dances were now held at St Stephen's Hall, the Nelson Room at the *Angel Hotel* on Broad Street, the *Eagle and Child* on Corve Street, Ludford Parish Room, the Picture House Cafe and in the pavilions at the Castle Tennis and Bowling Club, and the Burway Cricket and Hockey Club. New purpose-built dance venues also came on the scene to cater for the upsurge in demand. In 1928 the Winter Garden was opened in the Bull Ring at numbers 12 and 13, complete with a grand electric, self playing pianola in the lounge and an Aeolian organ that played orchestral music using a paper roll system. There was a maple block dance floor with surround seating in which to recline between dances. All was set in a simulated rock garden complete with classical statues. The whole:

> *'Was tastefully decorated and the lighting effects were carried out on a magnificent scale. Twilight dances were indulged in whilst the rockeries were illuminated with fairy lamps and the large revolving centre bowl gave a wonderful effect.'*[47]

In 1934 yet another new dance venue was opened at the Central Hall off Upper Galdeford. This building, originally a malthouse, then a chapel of ease and finally a furnishing showroom, was renovated and redecorated over two years by 'prominent men of the district.' The dance section was 60ft by 16ft with a sprung floor. A large anteroom, and ladies and gentlemen's cloakrooms could be found and the whole was supplied with electricity and heating.[48]

A further upsurge in dance venues occurred during the Second World War when thousand of troops were billeted in and around the town at some time or other. 1941 saw 12,000 dancers visiting Ludlow Town Hall alone in just six months and this figure increased as the war progressed. As well as the usual places, dances could now be found at the Women's Club off Quality Square, at the *Blue Boar* on Mill Street, at the *Compasses Inn* at the top of Corve Street and even at the Prisoner of War Camp that was situated at the Sheet. As Betty

Currie admitted: 'We went anywhere for a dance.'[49] Girls employed on shifts carrying out war work had to be inventive to manage to squeeze in dancing either before or after work. Betty Hince explained that when on an afternoon/evening shift 'before coming back we sneaked out to the toilet to get changed so we could go to a dance straight off the bus.' When the night shift was worked, Betty would attend a dance for the first half hour before catching the works bus, so important was dancing in her social life at the time.[50] Alongside the proliferation of local dances came the need for local dance bands. They reached double figures in the 1930s including Mrs Sherry and the Melody Makers, Will Jones and his Harmony Aces, Fred Lawton and his Band and Al Durrant's Blue Boys.[51]

The dance experience also underwent change during the interwar years and soon catered for different generations. Dances combined with whist drives became very popular and widespread. At one, organised by Ludlow Football Club in 1926, 384 people sat down at 96 tables to play competitive cards. In 1933, 328 people sat down at 82 tables. When this competition ended many stayed for the dance that followed though others set off for home. It was now that many of the younger generation arrived, increasing the total number of dancers to 500 with 300 still on the dance floor at 3.30am.[52] Young people would also flood into Ludlow from the surrounding countryside.

At the Central Hall 'many of the younger element of surrounding towns and villages made the journey to Ludlow especially for the dances.' As a result, a special bus was put on at 2am to take the dancers back to Bromfield, Onibury and Craven Arms.[53] Further evidence that working-class youth made up a large proportion of inter war dancers can be seen in court cases that came up before the local magistrates. When two young men were charged with damaging decorations at the Winter Garden, their occupations were given as a gas fitter and a labourer, whilst those of the two main witnesses were a

Dance halls proliferated in Ludlow to cater for the growing need of the populace to dance. The Charlton Arms Hotel at Ludford Bridge had one with a verandah overlooking the river where couples could relax after their exertions.
(Courtesy of Graham (Floyd) Wilson Lloyd)

postman and a plasterer. When a 17-year-old girl, working as a maid, was accused of stealing money from her employer, the police claimed that she had 'a craze for dancing and that she would go to any lengths to get money to attend dances.'[54]

The dress code at dances continued to undergo change and this was another factor that encouraged all classes to participate. Flannel dances became popular in the town from 1928 when the first was held at the Winter Garden. At such dances dress was casual, with flannel trousers and open necked shirts accepted as regards the men and dresses and skirts for the women. As well as encouraging more to go dancing, such dress allowed greater freedom of movement for energetic dances such as the Charleston and later the Jitterbug. Flannel

To cater for the many dances held each week, the number of local bands increased dramatically. One such was Fury's Dance band seen here practising at the Town Hall. Note the young man in short trousers. It was never too early to learn.

(Courtesy of Shropshire Museum Service)

dances immediately became very popular and they were soon being held at the Raven Lane Music Room and even at the Town Hall.[55]

It was not only cinemas that gave people a taste of another world away from a drab domestic environment. Dances often took place in colourful surroundings and not only at the exotic Winter Gardens. At a Ludlow and District Motor Club dance at the Town Hall, the room 'had been decorated to give it quite a motoring air… badges of the club had been placed around the hall and photographs of racing cars were plentifully distributed around the walls, whilst the stage was decorated with the club colours – dark blue, light blue and white.'[56]

Competitions and other forms of entertainment were also to be enjoyed. Spot prizes could be won at most dances whilst at others special events were held during a break in dancing. At one dance at the Town Hall in 1933, a Miss

Ludlow competition was held halfway through the evening, with the winner going on to an event in Shrewsbury where a Miss Shropshire would be chosen prior to competing in a national contest. At the following year's competition, thirteen girls took part in the final parade up and down the dance floor hoping to be chosen.[57] During the usual dancing at the Winter Garden, the floor was often cleared 'and with effective spot-lighting shining on the centre of the Winter Garden floor, spectacular speciality dances were performed by members of the cabaret show in beautiful costumes.'[58] At a Town Hall dance just after the end of the Second World War a hairstyle

1928 saw the introduction of flannel dances to Ludlow with the first being held at the exotic Winter Garden in the Bull Ring. Flannel trousers and open necked shirts for men and skirts for ladies meant that all could attend a dance without feeling out of place.
(Courtesy of LHRG Archive)

competition for the female dancers was one of the attractions with three prizes being awarded: most original hairstyle, most natural, and the most attractive.[59]

The arrival of dancing schools in the town helped open up dancing to a wider cross section of the people. Prior to the First World War, three private dancing schools advertised for clients in the local newspaper: one on Broad Street, one on Corve Street and one on Raven Lane. After the war further schools opened. A Miss Leonie Morris offered lessons at the

The Town Hall became the main venue for dances. Though set for a dinner in this photograph the size and splendour of the ballroom can be appreciated. (Courtesy of Shropshire Museum Service)

Town Hall as did a Mrs Brian Hatton. Miss Kathleen Short gave lessons at the Picture House Café or you could attend the Rosa Hubbard School of Dancing at 57, Broad Street. Miss Grace Dovey also offered instruction at the Picture House Café, then at 25, Broad Street and finally in the Nelson Room at the *Angel Hotel.* Dance classes could also be had at the skating rink on Lower Broad Street every Thursday and Saturday. Here, for just nine pence, two hours of instruction could be obtained. Lessons were not just for beginners. New dances such as the Foxtrot, Charleston, Tango and the New York Blues could be mastered.[60]

Novelty dances that could easily be picked up by dancers with various skill levels were introduced and enjoyed on local dance floors. In 1938 the Lambeth Walk, and Knees Up Mother Brown swept the nation and reached Ludlow with the Hokey Cokey soon following. But the greatest change came with the arrival of American troops to the town, prior to D Day, invading the local dance floors and bringing with them the Jitterbug. The local dance experience would never be the same again. One former young dancer recalled that 'most Americans did the jitterbug … you went over their shoulders and under their legs.' Yet another remembers her amazement at seeing dances that up until then had only been witnessed on the cinema screen. 'We stood there with our eyes popping.' The scene was set for the post-war introduction of dances such as the Jive.[61]

Dance floor etiquette also underwent change. A regular dancing column in the *Ludlow Advertiser,* which began in 1946, answered questions about what was now acceptable. When asked 'Could a lady turn down a dance request and if so can she then accept another one for the same dance?' the answer was yes to both questions and the reason given was female emancipation.[62]

By 1950, patterns of leisure had changed. The upper-class penchant for hunting and shooting had gone on mainly undisturbed. The middle-class, however, whilst at first trying to bring the working classes within the fold of its pursuits, had retreated behind 'respectable' barriers forming their own clubs and societies. As for the working classes, though efforts by the middle class to tame their more boisterous pastimes had been partially successful, attempts to inculcate team spirit and sportsmanship had not fully succeeded. Working-class leisure happily absorbed the introduction of sports such as association football, and pigeon racing and then had welcomed with open arms the coming of mass entertainment in the form of the cinema and the dance hall. These latter two entrants into working-class culture changed the lives of many wives and daughters in this section of society. For many years, upper and middle-class women had been able to enjoy leisure time and take part in sporting activities. Now many more women were allowed to begin to shake off the shackles of domestic drudgery and enjoy the freedom of entertainment outside the home.

All now enjoyed increasing leisure though social class still drew division lines as it had one hundred years before.

Footnotes

CHAPTER 1

1 *Eddowes Journal* 28 March 1860 and *Ludlow Advertiser* 30 April 1910.
2 *The Pubs of Ludlow and Neighbouring Villages* by Tony Hobbs (Logaston 2002) pp129-130.
3 Transcript of conversation with Diana Croft on Jeremy Sandford's Fan Club website.
4 Ludlow Hunt in Caynham by Rupert Inglesant (20003) on Caynham Village website and *Ludlow Advertiser* 19 March 1892.
5 *Ludlow and Leominster Herald* 31 December 1875 and *Ludlow Advertiser* 7 November 1891.
6 'The Hawkstone Otter Hunt' by Hugh L Heber Perry in *Badminton Magazine of Sports and Pastimes* Vol. 2 Issue 9 April 1896 pp. 463-475; *The Tatler* 20 May 1903 and *Ludlow Advertiser* 22 September 1894.
7 *Ludlow Advertiser* 2 November 1929.
8 *Eddowes Journal* 31 December 1862 and *Ludlow Advertiser* 10 February 1906.
9 *Ludlow Advertiser* 31 December 1892 and 7 January 1905.
10 *Wellington Journal* 19 December 1868 and *Ludlow Advertiser* 22 February 1895, 8 January 1898, 24 February 1906 and 14 February 1914.
11 *Ludlow Advertiser* 29 July 1925 and 16 January 1926.
12 *Ludlow Advertiser* 3 December 1927.
13 *Ludlow Advertiser* 11 May and 22 June 1907.
14 *Ludlow Advertiser* 29 April 1905 and 19 February 1921.
15 Ludlow Advertiser 30 March 1934.
16 Ludlow Advertiser 18 August 1906.
17 *Ludlow Advertiser* 21 June 1902.
18 *Hereford Times* 16 February 1839.
19 *Hereford Times* 24 February 1844.
20 *Hereford Times* 16 February 1839.
21 *Hereford Times* 3 March 1838.
22 *Shrewsbury Chronicle* 21 March 1851.
23 *Shrewsbury Chronicle* 11 February 1853.
24 *Ludlow Advertiser* 27 September 1919.
25 *Ludlow Advertiser* April 1903.
26 *Hereford Times* 20 February 1864.
27 *Ludlow Advertiser* 19 October 1929 and oral evidence of Jean Parker granddaughter of James Charmer.
28 *Eddowes Journal* 17 November 1847.
29 *Hereford Journal* 9 November 1867.
30 *Ludlow Advertiser* 11 November 1899, 12 November 1904 and 17 November 1900.
31 *Ludlow Days* by Arthur Everall in Shropshire Archives ref. 7320/4/3.
32 *Ludlow Advertiser* 11 November 1905, 27 October 1906 and 11 November 1911.
33 *Hereford Times* 28 December 1878.
34 *Ludlow Advertiser* 7 January 1911.
35 *Ludlow Advertiser* 1 January 1927, 4 January 1930 and 1 January 1937.
36 Extract from diary of Francis Richard Southern dated 1 January 1852 in the LHRG collection.
37 *Ludlow Advertiser* 5 January 1901, 3 January 1914 and 7 January 1928.
38 *The Pubs of Ludlow* op.cit. p. 133.
39 *Ludlow Advertiser* 20 July 1907 and 12 May 1923.
40 *Eddowes Journal* 14 May 1844 and *Wellington Journal* 7 May 1881.
41 Evidence of a Wigmore resident in 1914 recalling the 19th century in papers of

David Lloyd in hands of the Ludlow Historical Research Group, *Shrewsbury Chronicle* 4 May 1866 and *Eddowes Journal* 6 May 1863.
42 *Eddowes Journal* 7 May 1862.
43 *Shrewsbury Chronicle* 4 May 1866.
44 *Ludlow Advertiser* 7 May 1910.
45 *Ibid* and *Eddowes Journal* 7 May 1862.
46 *Shrewsbury Chronicle* 6 May 1870.
47 *Ludlow Advertiser* 5 May 1894.
48 *Ludlow Advertiser* 5 March 1892.
49 *Wellington Journal* 11 April 1896 and *Ludlow Advertiser* 12 May 1906.
50 *Ludlow Advertiser* May 1901.
51 *Ludlow Advertiser* 16 February 1895, 3 February 1912, 7 January 1928 and 28 January 1933.
52 *Ludlow Advertiser* 3 January 1914 and 20 January 1912.
53 *Ludlow Advertiser* 29 January 1927 and 10 January 1914.

CHAPTER 2

1 *The Licensing Return for Ludlow 1901* in Shropshire Archives Ref. QC36.8. Also for what follows see *Pubs in Ludlow and the Neighbouring Villages* by Tony Hobbs (Logaston Press (2002).
2 *Ludlow Advertiser* 5 May 1906.
3 *Women Drinking Out in Britain in the early Twentieth Century* by David Gutzke (Manchester, 2013) and *Ludlow Advertiser* 22 February 1908 and 19 October 1912.
4 *Wellington Journal* 18 August 1866 and Police Charge Books 1865-72 and 1872-1882 in Ludlow Museum Resource Centre.
5 *Ludlow Advertiser* 19 October 1901 and 18 January 1902. *Eddowes Journal* 18 April 1860.
6 *Ludlow Advertiser* 31 August 1934.
7 Evidence of Betty Currie née Lloyd of Sandpits Avenue, born 1920.
8 Evidence of Cynthia Wiggins née Edward.
9 Oral evidence of Jean Parker grand-daughter of James Charmer.
10 *Hereford Journal* 12 December 1849.
11 *Eddowes Journal* 18 September 1878.
12 *Encyclopedia of Traditional Rural Sports* edited by Tony Collins et al (London, 2005) pp. 95-96 and Ludlow Advertiser 23 September and 21 October 1938.
13 *Ludlow Advertiser* 4 January 1946.
14 *Ludlow Advertiser* 27 October 1928.
15 *Ludlow Advertiser* 30 December 1905.
16 *Ludlow Advertiser* 19 July 1890, 13 July 1893 and 10 October 1898; *Gloucester Citizen* 6 July 1900.
17 *Ludlow Advertiser* 17 August 1934.
18 *Ludlow Advertiser* 30 June and 23 December 1906.
19 *Ludlow Advertiser* 31 December 1926 and 9 April 1927.
20 *Ludlow Advertiser* 15 March 1890, 30 July 1892 and 3 October 1903. Also see Hobbs, *Pubs in Ludlow* Op cit.
21 *Ludlow Advertiser* 11 November and 30 August 1890 and 28 October 1899.
22 *Ludlow Advertiser* 27 May and 3 June 1911.
23 *Ludlow Advertiser* 27 August 1932.
24 *Ludlow Advertiser* 8 January 1898.
25 *Wellington Journal* 30 May 1896.
26 *Ludlow Advertiser* 13 July 1912 and 1 July 1911.
27 *Ludlow Advertiser* 4 April 1908, 20 April 1907 and 21 August 1900.
28 *Ludlow Advertiser* 30 May 1908.
29 *Ludlow Advertiser* 1 November 1924 and 26 September 1925.
30 *Ludlow Advertiser* 17 Nov 1906, 12 Oct 1907; 27 April 1912 and 17 Sept 1927.

31 Evidence of Phil Jones born 1932 and lived on the Bromfield Road.
32 *Ludlow Advertiser* 14 February 1947.
33 *Ludlow Advertiser* 1947.
34 *Ludlow Advertiser* 24 June 1905 and 8 March 1913.
35 *Ludlow Advertiser* 27 June 1925.
36 *Ludlow Advertiser* 28 Jan 1905, 3 Dec 1898, 5 April 1890 and 15 Oct 1892.
37 *Ludlow Advertiser* 6 September 1890, 5 September 1891 and 1 September 1894.
38 *Ludlow Advertiser* 12 July and 2 August 1902.
39 *Ludlow Advertiser* 6 May 1905.
40 *Ludlow Standard* 27 November 1931.
41 *Ludlow Advertiser* 18 May 1907, 22 February 1908 and *An Alphabet of Ludlow Pubs* by Harry Baker (privately published 1983).
42 *Ludlow Advertiser* 12 February 1937.
43 *Ludlow Advertiser* 12 September 1903 and 1 May 1905.
44 *Eddowes Journal* 21 January 1863 and *Ludlow Advertiser* 24 September 1875 and 15 November 1884.
45 *Ludlow Advertiser* 15 November 1946.
46 *Ludlow Advertiser* 25 June 1862 and 4 March 1905 and *Wellington Journal* 1 November 1882 and 20 October 1883.
47 *Ludlow Advertiser* 19 December 1925, 28 August 1920 and 23 September 1922.
48 *Ludlow Advertiser* 31 January 1925 and 10 November 1925 and 11 December 1926.
49 *Ludlow Advertiser* 1 January and 11 October 1924.
50 *The English Pub: A History* by Peter Hughes (London, 1994) and *Ludlow Advertiser* 3 February 1928.
51 *Ludlow Advertiser* 14 February 1941.

CHAPTER 3

1 *Eddowes Journal* 3 September 1862.
2 *Ludlow Advertiser* 27 August 1892.
3 Philip B Cliff, *The Rise and Development of the Sunday School Movement in England 1780-1980* (Redhill, 1986) Chapter 12.
4 *Ludlow Advertiser* 23 October 1909 and 8 October 1910.
5 *Ludlow Advertiser* 27 May 1905 and 8 April 1911.
6 *Eddowes Journal* 21 January 1863, *Wellington Journal* 16 October 1869 and Ludlow and *Leominster Herald* 24 September 1875.
7 *Ludlow and Leominster Herald* 23 October 1875 and *Ludlow Advertiser* 25 October 1884.
8 *Ludlow Advertiser* 11 January 1913, 10 May 1910 and 4 March 1911.
9 *Ludlow Advertiser* 28 December 1912 and 7 December 1912.
10 *Ludlow and Leominster Herald* 8 October 1875.
11 *Ludlow Advertiser* 12 February and 5 May 1910.
12 *Wellington Journal* 14 August 1869 and 17 August 1867.
13 *Ludlow Advertiser* 12 August 1905.
14 *Ludlow Advertiser* 6 November 1909, 4 June 1910 and 11 April 1911.
15 *Ludlow Advertiser* 2 March 1912 and 3 September 1910.
16 *Ludlow Advertiser* 26 November 1910 and 10 May 1913.
17 *South Shropshire's First World War* by Derek Beattie (Logaston, 2014) pp. 21-22.
18 See 'The development of Muscular Christianity in Victorian Britain and beyond' by Nick Watson, Stuart Weir and Stephen Friend in Journal of Religion and Society (Vol. 7 (2005). Also *Sport and the British* by Richard Holt (Oxford, 1992) pp.86-90.
19 *Century of Change 1900-2000* Robert Burns & David Lloyd (Merlin Unwin Books, 2000).
20 *Ludlow Advertiser* 17 December 1910 and 22 September 1923.
21 *Ludlow Advertiser* 12 March 1898 and 1 June 1907.
22 *Ludlow Advertiser* 17 September 1890 and 31 August 1895.

23 *Ludlow Advertiser* 24 May 1930.
24 *Eddowes Journal* 19 March 1863 and Ludlow Advertiser 2 November 1929.
25 *Ludlow Advertiser* 1 and 8 October 1910.
26 *Shrewsbury Chronicle* 27 August 1869 and *Eddowes Journal* 2 May 1866.
27 *Ludlow and Leominster Herald* 27 August 1875.
28 *Ludlow Advertiser* 30 September 1911.
29 *Ludlow Advertiser* 3 January 1925, 7 and 28 January 1933, 23 April 1934 and 30 October 1936. *Ludlow Standard* 21 April 1933 and a collection of boxing programmes in the possession of Maggie Wright.
30 *Ludlow Standard* 25 August 1933.
31 *Ludlow Advertiser* 1 June 1898 and 9 December 1905.
32 *Ludlow Advertiser* 19 March 1904, 7 June 1930, 25 May 1934 and 27 November 1936.
33 *Ludlow Advertiser* 5 October and 21 December 1907.
34 *Ludlow Advertiser* 3 February and 31 March 1923.
35 *Ludlow Advertiser* 30 March 1929 and 16 April 1937.
36 *Ludlow Advertiser* 16 December 1938.
37 *Ludlow Advertiser* 19 February and I December 1933.
38 *Ludlow Standard* 31 May 1940, 17 January and 14 March 1941.
39 *Ludlow Advertiser* 2 April 1940, *Ludlow Standard* 25 April and12 September 1941 and *Ludlow Advertiser* 20 September 1946.

CHAPTER 4

1 *Ludlow Advertiser* 6 August 1892, 11 August 1894 and 10 August 1907.
2 *Ludlow Advertiser* 21 August 1936.
3 *Ludlow Advertiser* 27 October 1894 and 1 November 1919.
4 *Ludlow Advertiser* 14 July 1923.
5 *Ludlow Advertiser* 7 July 1900.
6 *Eddowes Journal* 15 August 1860 and *Wellington Journal* 8 June 1867.
7 *Eddowes Journal* 18 June 1845 and 15 July 1845 and *Shrewsbury Chronicle* 22 July 1862.
8 *Ludlow Advertiser* 22 February 1890, 9 April 1892 and 23 August 1890.
9 *Ludlow Advertiser* 29 April 1905.
10 *Ludlow Advertiser* 27 July 1912 and 6 July 1912.
11 *Ludlow Advertiser* 26 June 1926, 18 June 1929, 28 April 1928 and 27 August 1929.
12 *Worcester Herald* 16 August 1834, *Wellington Journal* and *Shrewsbury News* 25 August 1883, *Ludlow Advertiser* 25 October 1884, *Birmingham Daily Post* 2 August 1884 and *Ludlow Advertiser* 17 June 1905.
13 *Wellington Journal*
14 *Shropshire Chronicle* 16 August 1867 and *Eddowes Journal* 21 August 1867.
15 *Ludlow Advertiser* 11 May 1895, 18 August 1894 and 29 July 1905.
16 *Ludlow Advertiser* 25 May 1922 and 18 April 1931.
17 *Ludlow Advertiser* 13 November 1936 and 7 May 1937.
18 *Hereford Times* 2 August 1854 and *Ludlow Advertiser* 10 October 1908 and 2 August 1913.
19 *Ludlow Advertiser* 14 September 1912 and 30 October 1920.
20 *Ludlow Advertiser* 9 August 1930.
21 *Ludlow Advertiser* 5 July and 2 August 1900.
22 *Ludlow Advertiser* 24 June 1911, 27 March 1920 and 26 November 1928.
23 *Ludlow Advertiser* 14 June 1930.
24 *Ludlow Advertiser* 31 January 1936.
25 See Ludlow Hockey Club Centenary Booklet 1885/6 – 1995/6 compiled by Roger Furniss (privately published).
26 *Ludlow Advertiser* 30 November 1901, 7 September 1907, 9 December 1922 and 27 September 1924.

27 *Wellington Journal* 25 May 1867.
28 Edwards, David, *Ludlow RFC: 75 Years 1934-2009* (privately published, 2009).
29 *Ludlow Advertiser* 19 November 1892, 14 February 1891 and 5 February 1910.
30 *Ludlow Advertiser* 12 August 1882.
31 *Ludlow Advertiser* 6 and 13 April 1912.
32 *Ludlow Advertiser* 28 March 1891 and 11 May and 6 July 1895.
33 *Ludlow Advertiser* 3 June 1899.
34 *Ludlow Advertiser* 16 September 1899.
35 *Ludlow Advertiser* 2 November 1895 and 5 September 1908.
36 *Ludlow Advertiser* 18 Oct 1919, 3 Aug 1920, 13 Sept 1924 and 25 June 1927.
37 *Ludlow Advertiser* 31 May and 14 June 1930.
38 *Ludlow Advertiser* 3 December 1932, 15 August 1933, 21 September 1934, 26 January 1934, 6 April 1934 and 4 January 1935. *Ludlow Standard* 9 August 1935.
39 *Ludlow Advertiser* 16 September 1897.
40 *Ludlow Standard* 30 October 1931 and Holt, Richard, *Sport and the British* op.cit. pp. 199-201.
41 *Ludlow Advertiser* 21 May, 16 June, 2 and 16 July 1932. Also Coburn, Oliver, *Youth Hostel Story: the first twenty years in England and Wales* (London, 1950).
42 *Ludlow Advertiser* 23 January 1892.
43 *Ludlow Advertiser* 15 March and 6 December 1890 and 21 March 1891.
44 *Ludlow Advertiser* 1 November 1892.
45 Ibid.
46 *Ludlow Advertiser* 7 May and 4 June 1910.
47 *Ludlow Advertiser* 20 October 1910 and 4 and 25 April 1911.
48 *Ludlow Advertiser* 16 September 1911.
49 *Ludlow Advertiser* 14 March and 5 September 1931.
50 See Hurlock, Richard, Ludlow Heritage News No 67 Autumn/Winter 2017.
51 Shrewsbury Chronicle 15 June 1855, 3 March 1868 and 3 September 1875.
52 *Ludlow Advertiser* 14 February 1885
53 *Ludlow Advertiser* 20 January 1894.
54 *Ludlow Advertiser* 12 April 1890.
55 *Ludlow Advertiser* 24 February 1900 and 13 October 1928.
56 *Shrewsbury Chronicle* 7 October 1864, *Wellington Journal* 16 January 1869 and *Ludlow Advertiser* 10 February 1894.
57 *Ludlow Advertiser* 31 March 1894 and 3 May 1930.

CHAPTER 5

1 *Ludlow Advertiser* 28 June 1890, 20 June 1891 and 8 June 1901.
2 *Ludlow Advertiser* 12 July 1924, 4 July 1925 and 19 May 1928.
3 *Ludlow and Leominster Herald* 14 April 1876 and *Ludlow Advertiser* 31 March 1906.
4 *Ludlow Days* by Arthur Everall in Shropshire Archives ref. 7320/4/3.
5 *Ludlow Advertiser* 14 May 1910 and 14 May 1921.
6 *Ludlow Advertiser* 7 July 1894 and 10 September 1898.
7 *Ludlow Advertiser* 3 June and 8 July 1905.
8 *Ludlow Advertiser* 28 June 1930.
9 *Ludlow Advertiser* 11 November 1938.
10 *Ludlow Advertiser* 3 June, 12 August, 17 June and 15 July 1905.
11 *Ludlow Advertiser* 10 Nov 1906, 30 March 1907, 7 July 1913 and 7 June 1930.
12 Oral Evidence of Kate Deeley born 1929 whose father was a farmer and butcher on Clee Hill.
13 *Ludlow Advertiser* 29 July and 2 September 1905, 4 August 1906 and 31 August 1907.
14 *Ludlow Advertiser* 8 August 1908, 31 July 1909, 27 August 1910 and 5 August 1911.
15 *Ludlow Advertiser* 18 April 1914.
16 *Ludlow Advertiser* 22 July 1898, 2 August 1902, I August 1903, 29 July 1911

and 13 September 1930.
17 *Ludlow Advertiser* 3 August 1894.
18 *Ludlow and Leominster Herald* 1 October 1875.
19 *Ludlow Advertiser* 6 August 1904.
20 *Ludlow Advertiser* 6 August 1898, 12 August 1911, 21 July 1923 and 30 July 1927.
21 *Hereford Times* 27 July 1878.
22 *Ludlow Advertiser* 1 August 1863.
23 *Ludlow Advertiser* 9 August 1890.
24 *Ludlow Advertiser* 19 May 1894.
25 *Ludlow Advertiser* 7 October 1905, 11 August 1906, 5 September 1908 and 27 September 1913.
26 *Ludlow Advertiser* 26 May 1923 and 7 and 14 June 1924.
27 *Ludlow Advertiser* 21 June 1913, 21 August 1920, 21 June 1924 and 28 April 1933.
28 *Ludlow Advertiser* 16 March 1929, 30 August 1930 and 6 October 1933.
29 *Ludlow Advertiser* 1 August 1931, 9 July 1932, 4 August 1933 and 7 August 1936.
30 Official programme of the event (published 1934) in author's possession.
31 *Wellington Journal* 9 October, 13 March and 13 November 1869, *Ludlow and Leominster Herald* 18 February 1876 and 30 October 1875.
32 *Ludlow Advertiser* 9 September 1911, 3 July 1912 and 15 July 1905.
33 *Ludlow Advertiser* 24 February and 12 March 1912.
34 *Ludlow Advertiser* 29 November 1924 and 10 August 1912.
35 For history of the early cinema see for example: Hill, Jeffrey, *Sport, Leisure and Culture in the 20th Century* (Basingstoke, 2002), Jones, Stephen C, *Workers at Play: A Social and Economic History of Leisure* (London, 1986) and Pugh, Martin, *We Danced all Night: A Social History of Britain Between the Wars* (London, 2009).
36 *Ludlow Advertiser* 10 August, 17 August 1912 and 8 February and 8 March 1913.
37 *Ludlow Advertiser* 12 April and 12 July 1913.
38 *Ludlow Advertiser* 27 November 1920, 23 July and 29 October 1921, 30 January and 20 February 1932 and 29 September 1933.
39 *Ludlow Advertiser* 17 September 1932, 2 February 1934 and 7 June 1930.
40 *Ludlow Advertiser* 10 January, 11 September 1920 and 26 March, 13 August 1921.
41 *Ludlow Advertiser* 30 August 1935, 23 September and 7 October 1938.
42 Shropshire Archives 6683/3/399/40 Letter to Lady Rouse Boughton dated July 1944.
43 *Ludlow Advertiser* 9 August 1930.
44 *Ludlow Advertiser* 30 October 1926 and 24 August 1934.
45 Evidence of Eileen Pearce (née Reynolds) born 1923 whose family lived at Warrington Gardens.
46 *Ludlow Advertiser* 2 January 1892, 28 December 1908, 20 January 1912 and 18 April 1914.
47 *Ludlow Advertiser* 21 January and 11 February 1928.
48 *Ludlow Advertiser* 9 November 1934.
49 Evidence of Betty Currie (née Lloyd) born 1920 of Sandpits Avenue.
50 Evidence of Betty Hince (née Nash) born 1924 of Old Street and Sandpits Avenue.
51 Various advertisements in *Ludlow Advertiser* 1934.
52 *Ludlow Advertiser* 30 January 1926 and 7 January 1933.
53 *Ludlow Advertiser* 7 December 1934.
54 *Ludlow Advertiser* 27 July 1934 and 25 November 1938.
55 *Ludlow Advertiser* 19 May and 7 July 1928.
56 *Ludlow Advertiser* 31 August 1934.
57 *Ludlow Advertiser* 10 August 1934.
58 *Ludlow Advertiser* 13 December 1930.
59 *Ludlow Advertiser* 29 March 1946.
60 *Ludlow Advertiserr* 17 February 1912, 10 September 1921 and 3 September 1927.
61 Evidence of Betty Currie *op.cit.* and Vera Ingram (née Taylor) born 1926 of Wheatcommon Lane, Richards Castle.
62 *Ludlow Advertiser* 29 March 1946.

Index

Other Shropshire publications by Merlin Unwin Books

for more details see
www.merlinunwin.co.uk

How the Other Half Lived
Ludlow's working classes 1850-1960
Derek Beattie

It Happened in Shropshire
Bob Burrows

A Shropshire Lad
A.E.Housman

A Year in Shropshire
Mike & John Hayward

Shropshire - from dawn to dusk
John & Jike Hayward

Nearest Earthly Place to Paradise
The Literary Landscape of Shropshire

A Most Rare Vision
Shropshire from the Air
Mark Sisson

Myddle
The life & times of a Shropshire farmworker's daughter in the 1920s
Helen Ebrey

The Temptation & Downfall of the Vicar of Stanton Lacy
Peter Klein

Beneath Safer Skies
A child evacuee in Shropshire
Anthea Toft